Anonymous

Victoria: It's History, Resources And Prospects

An Exhibition Memorial 1888 - 1889

Anonymous

Victoria: It's History, Resources And Prospects
An Exhibition Memorial 1888 - 1889

ISBN/EAN: 9783744692038

Printed in Europe, USA, Canada, Australia, Japan

Cover: Foto ©ninafisch / pixelio.de

More available books at **www.hansebooks.com**

VICTORIA:

ITS

HISTORY, RESOURCES AND PROSPECTS.

AN

𝕰𝖝𝖍𝖎𝖇𝖎𝖙𝖎𝖔𝖓 𝕸𝖊𝖒𝖔𝖗𝖎𝖆𝖑.

(1888-89.)

𝕸𝖊𝖑𝖇𝖔𝖚𝖗𝖓𝖊:
SANDS & McDOUGALL LIMITED, PRINTERS, COLLINS STREET WEST.
MDCCCLXXXVIII.

CONTENTS.

	PAGE
CHAPTER I.— Early History of Victoria	5
CHAPTER II.— Population and Growth of the Leading Cities	22
CHAPTER III.— Metallic Resources and their Development	33
CHAPTER IV.— Agriculture	44
CHAPTER V.— Vine Culture	62
CHAPTER VI.— Dairy Produce	70
CHAPTER VII.— Wool	76
CHAPTER VIII.— Commerce and Finance	86
CHAPTER IX. Development of Manufactures	99
CHAPTER X.— Social Statistics: Birth, Marriage, and Death Rates. Education, Schools, and University. Railways, Telegraph and Post Offices. Religious Statistics. Cost of Living. Victoria as a Field for Settlement	110

VICTORIA

Its History, Resources and Prospects.

CHAPTER I.

Early History of Victoria.

A DETAILED account of early discoveries by Spanish, Portuguese and Dutch navigators on the Australian coasts, north, east and west of the territory which now constitutes Victoria, will be studied with the deepest interest by all who desire to master the general history of "the Great South Land;" but we are exclusively concerned, in the present sketch, with the particular colony in which the Centennial International Exhibition of 1888 is held, and which is attracting visitors at this moment not only from all parts of Australia, but from many countries in the northern hemisphere.

It is universally admitted that the seaboard of Victoria was first observed by Captain Cook at Point Hicks, now called Cape Everard, in Gippsland, situated between Cape Howe and Snowy River, when he was on his way up from New Zealand to examine the coast-line of the mysterious continent.

It was on the morning of the 19th April, 1770, that Cook's first lieutenant sighted the promontory just mentioned, which continues to bear the name of the discoverer. Gabo Island and Cape Howe were seen by Cook himself on the same day. But more than a quarter of a century was allowed to elapse before further examination was made of the southern trend of Australia, which was still supposed to extend to the forty-third parallel of latitude. The first Europeans who touched the soil of Victoria were Clarke, the supercargo, and the crew of the *Sydney Cove*, wrecked early in 1797, south of Cape Howe. On the 4th January, 1798, the Western Port inlet was entered by the intrepid Bass, who was accompanied by Matthew Flinders, then only a midshipman. The stay of Bass in that locality, however, was not prolonged beyond thirteen days, when circumstances obliged him to retrace his steps to Port Jackson, and he departed under the impression that the southern portion of Australia was connected with Van Diemen's Land, and that the passage now known as Bass' Straits was only a deep bight.

To Lieutenant Grant, of the brig *Lady Nelson*, belongs the honour of having defined the entire coast-line of Victoria for the first time, from Cape Bridgewater to Cape Schanck, in the year 1800. From this gallant adventurer Capes Northumberland, Bridgewater, Nelson, Solicitor, Sir W. Grant and Otway, with Mounts Schanck and Gambier, Laurence Road, and Lady Julia Percy Island, received the nomenclature by which they are still known. Portland Bay he called after the famous duke of Dutch descent, then one of the Secretaries of State. In the following year he surveyed the shores of Victoria from Wilson's Promontory to Western Port. Churchill's Island, in Western Port Bay, was visited by him, and on that spot he was reduced to the necessity of cultivating a garden with a coal-shovel, in the absence of any more convenient implement. It would appear that he formed a decidedly more accurate opinion of the region in question than some of the authorities at Sydney, and other officials, subsequently did, for he compared the beauty of the scenery to Devonshire and the Isle of Wight.

Grant, returning to England, was succeeded in the command of the *Lady Nelson* by Lieutenant John Murray, who reaped the first Victorian grain-crop from the seed which had been sown by his predecessor. On the 5th January, 1802, that gallant commander left Western Port with the intention of exploring the coast trending in a north-westerly direction, but was beaten back by adverse winds. Baffled in his attempt to enter what looked like an inlet, he despatched his first mate with five seamen to examine the place, and thus was brought to the knowledge of the world the existence of Port Phillip Bay, which is destined to play so momentous a part in the future triumphs of commerce and civilisation in the Southern Pacific. The launch containing the exploring party rounded the promontory familiar to us as Point Nepean, that designation being applied to it by the first officer of the *Lady Nelson* on the occasion referred to. On the 1st February the "Rip" was safely passed through, when the great inland sea expanded to the wondering gaze of the visitors. On the fourth of the same month they returned to their vessel to report what they had seen, and, eleven days afterwards, the *Lady Nelson* sailed through the Heads. Traces of the natives were visible in the numerous huts standing near the portion of the bay where Lieutenant Murray landed, and in the charred appearance of some hundreds of acres which had apparently been cleared by fire. Murray was as much struck with the pleasant aspect of the landscape as Grant had been with the Victorian coast-line off Gippsland. He describes the bay as a "noble harbour," and compares the scenery to that of Greenwich Park and Blackheath, "the hills and valleys rising and falling with inexpressible elegance." A conspicuous height on the eastern shore he designated "Arthur's Seat," from its likeness to the celebrated hill of that name overlooking the Scotch capital. The treacherous greeting given to the newcomers by the blacks came very near costing them their lives, and it became necessary, in self-defence, to give the aborigines a practical illustration of the power of the strange tubes pointing through the port-holes of the brig to vomit forth fire and destructive shot.

On the 9th of March, Murray took possession of the bay and its surroundings in the King's name, hoisting his emblematic bunting on Point Patterson, and firing rounds of small arms and artillery in honour of the occasion. On the 12th the vessel got back through the "Rip" on an ebb tide, and steered direct for Port Jackson.

The fate of the *Lady Nelson* forms a melancholy sequel to this narrative of the first visit of white men to the inlet at the head of which Victoria's capital was founded thirty-three years afterwards. In 1825, while engaged on a trading expedition in Torres Straits, she was seized by Malays, and it is believed that her crew was massacred; at least she was never heard of again.

Matthew Flinders, who has already been alluded to in his capacity as midshipman on board the vessel which had conveyed Dr. Bass to the South Pacific, entered Port Phillip Bay the very month after Murray quitted it. As no opportunity had occurred for communication between

EARLY HISTORY. 9

the two commanders, they were entirely ignorant of being in such close proximity to each other. Flinders sailed from Spithead in July, 1801, in command of the sloop-of-war *Investigator*, under instructions to make a complete survey of the Australian coast. Sir John Franklin, afterwards Governor of Tasmania, and still more distinguished as an Arctic explorer, served under Flinders as midshipman on the voyage referred to. Skirting the south-west coast of Victoria from Cape Bridgewater to Cape Otway, Flinders passed through the Heads into Port Phillip on 27th April, 1802, under the notion that he was in Western Port. He was soon undeceived, however, by the spectacle of a sheet of water so vast that its northern boundaries were far too remote to be noticeable, even from a hill which he ascended for the purpose of endeavouring to observe them. From You Yangs mountain, on the western side of the bay, he saw the plains of the interior, and caught a glimpse of those hills around the present Ballarat, which, 48 years later, yielded auriferous treasures so rich that the neighbourhood was reputed for a time a veritable El Dorado, both in Europe and America. He did not fail to note the superior grazing capabilities of the country, but was unable to discover any signs of fresh water, although, as was afterwards ascertained, there were three distinct sources of supply within a few miles of the mountain (now called Station Peak) which he had climbed. Flinders is entitled to high rank in the list of Australian explorers, not only for the services just described, but also as being the first who circumnavigated Australia, and claimed possession of its entire territory for the British crown.

The favourable report of Murray, confirmed by Flinders, induced Governor King to urge upon the Duke of Portland the desirableness of forming a settlement at Port Phillip. This suggestion was based not merely on the obvious fertility of the soil and the genial character of the climate, but also on the anxiety of His Excellency to checkmate the French, who had sent out the ship *Le Geographie* to explore the Australian coasts with the alleged object of planting a French colony somewhere close by. Pending the arrival from Downing Street of full authority to carry out his contemplated project, Governor King commissioned Mr. Charles Grimes, the Surveyor-General of New South Wales, and Lieutenant Charles Robbins, a naval officer, to perform a walking tour round Port Phillip harbour. This task was undertaken by these gentlemen in December, 1802. The leader of the expedition discovered the river Yarra on the 30th January, 1803, and it was ascended by him as far as Dight's Falls, Studley Park, on the 2nd of February. The party breakfasted on Batman's Hill, which has since been levelled to make way for the Spencer Street railway station, Melbourne. Happily the journal of the Grimes Expedition, kept by James Fleming, one of the assistant surveyors of the party, is preserved in the archives of the Colonial Secretary's Office at Sydney. In that document Mr. Fleming remarks:—" The most eligible place for a settlement that I have seen is on the Freshwater River [the Yarra]. In several places there are small tracts of good land, but they are without wood and water. The country in general affords excellent pasture and is thin of timber, which is mostly low and crooked." At the same time the course of the Saltwater River was traced from its *débouché* back to Keilor. Corio Bay was carefully examined, but the explorers kept too near the beach in their journey to admit of any acquaintance being made by them with the Barwon or the Moorabool. On

EARLY HISTORY.

the whole, the decision of the Surveyor, as the result of his circumambulation, was unfavourable to the vicinity of Port Phillip as a place of settlement. A different conclusion was arrived at, however, by the Colonial authorities in London, after considering the despatches of Governor King. Eight days subsequent to the discovery of the Yarra, Lieutenant-Colonel Collins was sent out from England in charge of a cargo of convicts, under the surveillance of a small armed force, to form a penal settlement on the shores of Port Phillip, corresponding to the one which had previously been established at Sydney Cove. The party, numbering 402 souls, comprised 15 Government officials, 9 officers of marines, 2 drummers and 39 privates, 5 soldiers' wives and 1 child, 307 convicts, with 12 married women and 1 child. They were conveyed in H.M.S. *Calcutta*, a ship of 1,200 tons, which was accompanied by the *Ocean*, a store ship of 481 tons, sailing from Spithead on the 24th April, 1803. The *Calcutta* called for stock, seed, and provisions at Teneriffe, Rio Janeiro, and Simon's Bay. The same vessel made the land about Port Phillip on the 9th October, and entered the harbour on the same day, the *Ocean* arriving two days sooner. A landing of the exiles was effected about eight miles from the Heads, near the site of the present watering-place, Sorrento. The choice of Collins for the command of such an expedition was singularly unfortunate, since proof is only too plain that he came out to Australia under a strong apprehension that his mission would result in failure. He appointed Lieutenant Tuckey, with two assistants, to survey the harbour in the *Calcutta's* launch; and, after spending nine days in this undertaking, Tuckey wrote of Port Phillip:—" The kangaroo seems to reign undisturbed lord of the soil, a dominion which he is likely to retain for ages." In a similar strain Collins, in his despatches to the Home Government, dwelt *ad nauseam* on "the disadvantages of Port Phillip," and the unsuitability of the bay itself, "when viewed in a commercial light," for the purposes of a colonial establishment; and he added a prediction, than which none was ever more signally falsified, that the place would never be "resorted to by speculative men!" While regretting on a certain occasion, during his stay in Sullivan's Bay, the necessity of employing hands to load the *Ocean* previous to his abandonment of the proposed settlement, he justifies his course on the ground that "the sooner we are enabled to leave this unpromising and unproductive country the sooner shall we be able to reap the advantages and enjoy the comforts of a more fertile spot." In this view Collins was strengthened by Governor King, who had altered his opinion under the influence of Grimes' representations, and in a letter to Collins dated from Port Jackson, 26th November, 1803, His Excellency writes— "It appears, as well by Mr. Grimes' and Mr. Robbins' survey, that Port Phillip is totally unfit for settlement in every point of view." Moved by the picture of desolation thus exhibited, Lord Hobart sent out instructions that the Collins settlement was to be broken up and transferred to the river Derwent, Van Diemen's Land. On the 24th January, 1804, Collins was not sorry to quit the despised bay in obedience to orders from London. The expedition remained on shore altogether fifteen weeks, and during that period there had been one birth, one marriage, and twenty-one deaths. The first child of European descent was born in Victoria on the 25th November, 1803, and was named William James Hobart Thorne. The first wedding took place on the 28th of the same month, between Richard Garrett, a convict, and Hannah Harvey, a free woman. The first death was that of John Skilhorne, a settler, on the 10th of October.

When it is remembered that the persistent depreciation of Port Phillip by Collins and others in authority was attended with its fortunate escape—however narrowly—from the taint of convictism, we can but regard the erroneous opinions which had been formed of the soil as a "blessing in disguise." Nevertheless, it cannot be denied that from the abortive attempt of Collins at settlement dates the prejudice indulged by a section of the Sydney people against the country, which has never been completely effaced, despite its marvellous strides in population, wealth and enterprise in the last forty years. How near the officers of the *Calcutta* were to ushering in the gold era—which, however, did not dawn for about thirty years later—is seen from the recorded fact that some of them found a sparkling substance in a sandy stream they had met with, which they thought to be gold.

For twenty years after the departure of the *Calcutta*, Victoria remained unvisited by a single ship, and untrodden by a white man's foot. Meanwhile, a limited patch of territory around Sydney had, during that interval, developed good agricultural capabilities. These pastoralists had more or less prospered, and flocks and herds had multiplied. The spirit of exploration was also active among the inhabitants of Port Jackson. In 1817, the head waters of the Macquarie were reached by Wentworth and Blaxland over the Blue Mountains. Evans brought to light the productive region now known as Bathurst Plains. Oxley journeyed along the banks of the Macquarie and the Lachlan, foreshadowing the discovery of a mighty stream, flowing in a south-west direction. But it was not

J. H. Nicholson, 65 William Street, Melbourne.

until 1824 that the Murray was seen for the first time by white men. Those who enjoyed this distinction were Hamilton Hume and W. C. Hovell, two stockmen, who in that year crossed the Australian Alps, discovered the Upper Murray, and passed into Victoria. Hume was a bold, persistent, and energetic bush traveller, and had been previously consulted by Sir Thomas Brisbane, in Sydney, in reference to an overland expedition to the south coast of New South Wales. The travellers started on the 3rd October, and on the 17th November crossed the Murray. On the 24th the Ovens River was met with and named; the head waters of the Goulburn were struck on 3rd December; King Parrot Creek was discovered on the 7th, and the shores of Corio Bay, near the present site of Geelong, on the 17th of the latter month. Hume was afterwards second in command to Captain Charles Sturt, and Hovell was attached to an expedition despatched from Sydney to Western Port by Governor Darling in December, 1826. The origin of the latter expedition—which consisted of detachments of the 3rd and 30th Regiments, despatched in H.M. ships *Fly* and *Dragon*—was a determination on the part of His Excellency to forestall a supposed design of the French to appropriate Western Port for colonising purposes. After a year's trial, however, the British settlement at that point was given up, partly because suspicion of the French had cooled down, and partly for the unsupported reason that the place was unfit for a penal settlement.

Captain Sturt's exploration of the Murray belongs to general geographical discovery in Australia. The next leading event, directly bearing on Victorian history, was the establishment of the first permanent settlement in Victoria by a few Englishmen who had experienced disappointment in respect to the capabilities of Western Australia and Van Diemen's Land. To the brothers Henty belongs the honour of being the first family who came to Victoria to stay. The Jason of these Argonauts was Edward Henty, who died in 1878, and whose memory is entitled to special respect as the real father of the colony. He was the son of Mr. Thomas Henty, banker and landowner in Sussex, who, with his sons, emigrated to Launceston, Tasmania, in 1831. Edward, being desirous of ascertaining by personal inspection what part of the coast was best adapted for settlement, visited Spencer's Gulf, and spent two months in examining the country. Bad weather drove his vessel, on her return passage to Launceston, for refuge into Portland Bay, 266 miles west of Port Phillip. The appearance of the country impressed Edward Henty favourably. He visited Portland again in 1833, bringing with him from Tasmania farm implements, vegetable seeds and fruit trees, supplied to him by his father. The first building erected in Victoria was Mr. Henty's wool store; the first dwelling was Richmond House, in which he resided at Portland, and where the first native Victorian of European descent, Richmond Henty, was born. Edward constructed the first plough, which was exhibited at the Victorian Agricultural Show of 1887, held in Melbourne, turned the first furrow, planted the first vine, milked the first cow, shod the first horse, and sheared the first sheep, in Victoria. His brother Stephen and he had been successful in whaling pursuits while at Launceston, and soon converted Portland into a whaling as well as a sheep and cattle station. Francis, a younger brother, who was a youth when he landed with his brother Edward in Victoria, resided in Melbourne at the date of our writing, and no name in the colony is more highly esteemed.

J. H. Nicholson, 65 William Street, Melbourne.

One of the surprises encountered by Major (afterwards Sir Thomas) Mitchell on his exploratory overland journey in 1836, from New South Wales to the southern country, was "a considerable farming establishment belonging to the Messrs. Henty," which he found in a region regarded by him as totally uninhabited by whites. After examining the Darling and Riverina districts, he turned southward on the 20th June, 1836, towards the junction of the Loddon and the Murray. Bending his course westward, he crossed the Avoca and the Wimmera, and climbed to the top of Mount William, overlooking a magnificent and variegated range of country, whose rare adaptation for agricultural and pastoral purposes justified him in denominating it *Australia Felix*. After discovering the beautiful valley of the Wannon, lying to the east of the river now known as the Glenelg, and which received its name from the explorer, Major Mitchell and his party reached Portland on the 20th August. His first thought was that the establishment of the Hentys was a nest of pirates, while that family, with quite as much justification, deemed Mitchell and his party a gang of bushrangers. Naturally, the satisfaction of hosts and guests was mutual in being undeceived. It is noteworthy that another infant settlement had taken root on the banks of the Yarra, of whose existence Mitchell had not been cognisant. Speaking of the view from the summit of Mount Macedon, to which he assigned the name it bears, he says:—"I could trace no signs of life about this harbour [*i.e.*, Port Phillip]. No stockyards, cattle, nor even smoke, although at the northern point of the bay I saw a mass of white objects which might have been either tents or vessels." Yet, upwards of a year previously, a settlement had been formed near the bay, and the foundations laid of the city of Melbourne.

Nicholson's Ear Drums Cure Deafness.

EARLY HISTORY. 17

The next notable figure identified with the early history of the colony was John Batman, who arrived from Van Diemen's Land at Port Phillip in May, 1835, and concluded a treaty with the natives for a grant of 600,000 acres of land, which, however, like many other schemes of a like kind proposed by immigrants, was unceremoniously disallowed by the Imperial Government. About eight years previously, John Batman and J. T. Gellibrand, of Launceston, asked for a grant of land at Western Port, with a view to following pastoral pursuits in that locality. The application, however, was summarily rejected by Governor Darling, to whom it was addressed. But the project went to sleep until Batman, in 1835, chartered a vessel at Launceston, and, in company with seven black fellows from Sydney, proceeded to Port Phillip. Following the track of Flinders, as laid down in a copy of a chart sketched by that commander, Batman ascended Station Peak, and looked down with admiration on the rolling and fertile country which Hume and Hovell had traversed. He then followed in part in the footsteps of Surveyor-General Grimes, ascending the Saltwater and Freshwater Rivers. The latter he called the Yarra Yarra, supposed to mean the "ever flowing." Meeting a body of natives, he arranged the contract before referred to for the transfer to himself and his heirs for ever of a large area of land, which included the present sites of Melbourne and Geelong and all their suburbs. The price to the natives by the intended buyer, for an estate considerably more than half a million acres in extent, was twenty pairs of blankets, thirty tomahawks, a hundred knives, fifty pairs of scissors, thirty looking-glasses, two hundred handkerchiefs, one hundred pounds of flour, and six shirts— to be paid down at once; and an annual value of one hundred pairs of blankets, one hundred knives, one hundred tomahawks, fifty suits of clothing, fifty pairs of scissors, and five tons of flour. The original document may be seen in the Melbourne Public Library. Another transaction, only somewhat less ambitious, was attempted by Batman with a tribe who claimed to be owners of a great domain in the vicinity of Corio Bay. He endeavoured to obtain from the latter possession of 100,000 acres in that district; but, as in the larger negotiation, the Imperial Government refused to ratify the bargain. His partners in the undertaking were C. Swanston, James Simpson, J. T. Gellibrand and J. H. Wedge, and ultimately the Governor of New South Wales allowed the Batman Syndicate £7,000 in remission of money actually due from them on land they had purchased at Port Phillip, in compensation for the claims which Governor Darling and the home authorities had cancelled, " recognising the services which the company had rendered in the colonisation of the country." Notwithstanding professions of goodwill by the aborigines, it turned out that they had hatched a plot for taking Batman's life, which was only frustrated by the interposition of " the wild white man," William Buckley, who had escaped from the short-lived settlement under Captain Collins in 1803, and who, after solitary wanderings, had lived among the natives as one of themselves for thirty years. When Batman met this almost naturalised blackfellow, he had lost all recollection of his native language, which was only to a very small extent brought to mind by him during the remainder of his life. He was held by the blacks to be an ancient and buried chief, risen from the dead, and was venerated accordingly. The sight of one of his own race, after so long and unbroken a period spent among

Nicholson's Ear Drums Cure Deafness.

savages, touched his sympathies. Hence the assistance he so seasonably rendered to Batman in a moment of peril.

Close upon the heels of Batman came John Pascoe Fawkner, another Launceston man, who in the same year organised an expedition for the colonisation of the same locality. Fawkner had served in some capacity on board the *Calcutta*, when Collins made unsuccessful efforts to found his settlement near Sorrento, and he consequently knew something of the harbour. For partners in the new immigration movement he had six other persons. He chartered in Tasmania the *Enterprise*, a 50-ton schooner, which entered Port Phillip Heads on the 16th August, 1835. The vessel was moored on the north bank of the Yarra, immediately opposite the site of the present Custom House, in Flinders Street, Melbourne. At that time the river was fringed with feathery scrub, and was not as yet tainted by the sewage of a great city. The *Enterprise* landed its cargo, consisting of horses, ploughs, pigs, furniture, and farming implements. Five acres were soon ploughed and planted with corn, fruit trees and vegetables. But Fawkner delayed his own coming until the following trip of the vessel. Five hundred sheep and fifty head of cattle arrived in the following month. John Aitken also brought a number of sheep about the same time, and depastured them on Mount Macedon. Fawkner "turned the first sod, built the first house, opened the first church, and started the first newspaper in the settlement." He may, therefore, claim to be the father of Melbourne, Batman being entitled to credit as the first coloniser of the shores of Port Phillip Bay. The first sermon was preached by the Rev. James Orton, a Wesleyan minister who came over with Batman in April, 1836, under the shade of the

J. H. Nicholson, 65 William Street, Melbourne.

Casuarina oaks on Batman's Hill. The settlement on the Yarra was now sufficiently advanced to call for governmental administration. A petition to that effect was agreed upon at a public meeting. Governor Bourke was solicited to appoint a resident magistrate at Port Phillip, and the prayer of the petitioners was conceded. Already 177 settlers from Van Diemen's Land had become inhabitants of the district, their stock and other property amounting to £110,000. Before the close of 1836 the population was materially increased. The resident magistrate appointed by Governor Bourke was Captain Lonsdale, and his duties were rendered specially arduous owing to the number of blacks within a circuit of thirty miles, being five times the number of whites under his magisterial jurisdiction. The first public-house was started by Fawkner at the corner of what is now William and Collins Streets, from which centre the city spread eastwards. The first houses, for the most part, were of wattle-and-dab, and to the east of Swanston Street all was wilderness. In 1837 Sir Richard Bourke came over from Sydney to visit the rising city, and encamped in the western part of the street called after him. Half-acre city allotments, put up at auction at £5 each—£7 being then deemed too high a price—were sold a few months afterwards at £25 to £100 each. The hut of Batman's shepherd stood where St. Francis' Cathedral is erected, in Elizabeth Street, and the first post-office was opened in a small brick building a little west of what is now Temple Court, in Collins Street West.

On the 4th February, 1839, Lord Glenelg, Secretary of State for the Colonies, appointed Mr. Charles Joseph Latrobe Superintendent of the District of Port Phillip, that office carrying with it the authority of Lieutenant-Governor.

Nicholson's Ear Drums Cure Deafness.

He erected a wooden house, which he had brought out with him from England, on sloping ground eastward of the city, upon which he saw fit to bestow the name of Jolimont. In August, 1850, an Imperial Act was passed erecting the district into a separate colony, Mr. Latrobe being appointed first Governor. In that year, which immediately preceded the one in which gold was discovered, the province of Port Phillip, not yet fifteen years old, had a revenue of £230 000, while its exports amounted to £760,000, and its population to 76,000. These figures are sufficient to show that the colony had ample resources to ensure its solid development, independently of the gold discoveries, which, nevertheless, so powerfully accelerated its expansion. What sanguine dreamer, in his wildest imaginings, could have anticipated, thirty-seven years ago, that Victoria, in the year 1888, should possess more than a million inhabitants; that the population of its capital and suburbs should reach 390,000; that the revenue of the colony should be £7,000,000 a-year; that the products of the western portion of the colony, first cultivated by the Hentys and the Robertsons, should have attained such large dimensions; and that Gippsland, discovered by Angus McMillan, who started on his tour of exploration from a station near the Snowy Mountains in January, 1840, with a stock-rider, should give promise of such splendid progress; that 1,800 miles of railways should be working, and paying to the bondholders who lent the money to build them full interest on the outlay, with a surplus to the good?

J. H. Nicholson, 65 William Street, Melbourne,

CHAPTER II.

Population and Growth of the Leading Cities.

MELBOURNE has risen, in the short space of fifty-three years, from the little farming village, established by Batman and Fawkner on the banks of the Yarra in 1835, to the position of the ninth city in the world, and handsome streets and buildings, which have been admired by visitors from all parts. Mr. Anthony Trollope described it as "one of the most successful cities on the face of the earth." Mr. G. A. Sala gave it a world-wide reputation as "Marvellous Melbourne."

The town of Melbourne, when fifteen months old, consisted of about 100 houses, amongst which were stores, inns, a gaol, a barrack, and a school-house. Some of the dwelling-houses were tolerable structures of brick. A few of the inhabitants were living in tents, or in hovels with thatched roofs, till they could provide themselves with better accommodation. The town allotments had been put up at £5 each, but some of them sold for from £25 to £100 each. The Bank of Australasia established a Melbourne branch in 1838, the officers who came over from Sydney making a voyage of six weeks' duration in a schooner. Victorian journalism had its birth in the

Nicholson's Ear Drums Cure Deafness.

same year, Mr. Fawkner's first newspaper, the *Advertiser*, being published in manuscript. The pastoralists who took up land to the north and west prospered, and the metropolitan settlement rapidly increased. Melbourne was made a city in 1849, and in the following year Port Phillip, as the district was called, had a revenue of £230,000; its exports amounted to £760,000; and its population was over 76,000. In February, 1851, the great bush fires occurred. Fertile districts were wasted, and there was a terrible destruction of life and property by the conflagrations, which culminated on "Black Thursday." In July of the same year the district of Port Phillip became the colony of Victoria. A few weeks afterwards the country was electrified by the gold discoveries, which were to have such an important effect on its advancement. Early in the following year immigrant ships had begun to arrive in large numbers—in one year alone 80,000 persons arrived—and the quiet town of Melbourne became a very bustling place.

Two remarkable developments which arose out of the crowded state of the metropolis were Canvas Town and Rag Fair. House accommodation became wholly inadequate to meet the requirements of the great multitude, and holders of tenements made enormous profits by letting portions of their mean dwellings at extraordinary high rents. Many persons not destitute of means were obliged to live in tents, while large numbers slept in the open air. A unique suburb sprang into existence on the south side of the Yarra, just beyond Prince's Bridge. It was improvised by the surplus population, who could not obtain shelter in overcrowded Melbourne. Its name—Canvas Town—describes its construction. It was pleasantly situated, commencing on a grassy slope, and was laid out in streets and lanes; the principal thoroughfares were crowded with boarding-houses and shops, all of canvas. The Government charged the occupant of each impromptu dwelling 5s. per week for the right to camp on the site. All sorts of people mingled together in this primitive township, and here many "new chums" took their first lesson in roughing it. After a time, however, the police gave so bad an account of the place that the Government determined on its suppression.

Another novel and interesting scene was the market which sprang into existence on the wharf, where most of the arrivals landed, in Flinders Street. The exorbitant rates charged for cart-hire and store-rent precluded many from removing their heavy luggage, which remained day after day piled up in huge heaps by the water-side. At length some of the immigrants devised a plan for its sale. An impromptu bazaar was opened; the sea-chests were placed back to back and arrayed in lines with the upturned lids strewed with the contents, so that the merchandise was fully exposed for inspection. A brisk trade soon sprang up, in which abundance of wearing apparel and household furniture was sold at "alarming sacrifices," as the exigencies of the times demanded the immediate disposal of all cumbrous articles. The low prices increased the popularity of this Rag Fair, as it was called, and the business became at last so considerable that, in response to the complaints of shopkeepers, the City Council ordered its discontinuance. In striking contrast to the efforts made by these new chums in getting rid of their superfluities in order to buy a suitable outfit for the diggings, were the dissipations and freaks of many returned diggers, who, having been lucky on the goldfields, were now recklessly squandering their quickly-acquired wealth. These extra-

POPULATION AND GROWTH.

vagant displays tended to quicken the movements of new arrivals in their preparations, and to keep up a constant flow of the population between the rich diggings and the town. In these days the streets of Melbourne were full of gum-tree stumps and deep ruts. The principal thoroughfare, Elizabeth Street, was for months in the year a flooded quagmire, in which, on one occasion, a waggon and team of horses were absolutely swallowed up, and bullock drays were daily bogged. Imported iron buildings and bark "humpies" were also common on every hand.

Melbourne is now one of the finest capitals in the world. Including its suburban municipalities, eighteen in number, all lying within a radius of ten miles of the Town Hall, it contains 371,630 inhabitants. It is well laid out, with wide and regular streets, with broad sidewalks, well-paved and lighted. Tree-planting in the streets has been extensively carried on, giving a pleasant shade, as well as being refreshing to the eye. The chief buildings are not only handsome, but many are of great architectural merit. The cathedrals and churches, schools, Parliament House, Treasury, Town Hall, Post Office, Law Courts, Customs House, University, Museum, Free Library, National Gallery, banks, clubs, theatres, and other public institutions, are worthy of special admiration. The banking corporations are settled in buildings which would adorn Threadneedle Street. The wharfs on the banks of the Yarra now give accommodation to large ocean-going steamers. The shops and warehouses are equal to those of leading cities in the Old World. Everything necessary to make life enjoyable can be procured in Melbourne, and the mansions in the fashionable suburbs are only less gratifying evidences of the prosperity of the people than the thousands of pleasant

J. H. Nicholson, 65 William Street, Melbourne.

cottages—many of them the freehold property of their occupants—to be seen on every road within a few miles of the city.

Any visitor to the colony must be struck with the perfect arrangements for water supply. Every house, down almost to the smallest cottage, has its bath-room. The most important reservoir is the Yan Yean, which is an artificial lake at the foot of the Plenty Ranges, nearly nineteen miles from Melbourne proper. A few years back complaints as to the quality of the water of the Yan Yean were numerous; but now, the water, though perhaps not quite pellucid, is perfectly safe and pure. The numerous parks and reserves and public gardens in and around Melbourne are heritages, sacred to the health and enjoyment of the people, which astonish the new-comer from crowded European cities, where one is taxed for space to breathe. This is above all a place for the people. In no large town of the world has a working man so many enjoyments as in Melbourne, or so many privileges. The whole country, as well as the metropolis, is dotted with free State schools. The Free Library, Museum, Picture Galleries, and the Botanic and Zoological Gardens afford free recreation and instruction to the labourer and mechanic, as well as to the clerk or shopman. Melbourne is plentifully furnished with provident, charitable, literary, scientific, religious and social institutions to suit all classes and creeds. In the matter of amusement the inhabitants of the metropolis are furnished with five theatres and several music halls, and there are numerous flourishing musical societies. There is also abundant provision for outdoor sports, which are always well patronised. Racing, cricket, lawn tennis, football, rowing, yachting, and bicycle riding are the most popular amusements. There are no more perfect arrangements of the kind in the world than those at the Melbourne Cricket Ground, where the members' pavilion is not only a grand-stand, but possesses dining, billiard, and bath-rooms. Melbourne possesses two first-class racecourses within a few minutes' ride by rail from the city. At Flemington the greatest race in Australia, the "Melbourne Cup," is run on the first Tuesday in November. From every part of the continent, people of all classes then flock to Victoria's metropolis. The "Cup Week" is the Carnival of Australia. If Flemington is like Epsom, Caulfield course may be said to be the Ascot of Melbourne. There is an annual attendance of not less than 100,000 well-dressed people at Flemington on Cup Day, and drunkenness and disorder are always conspicuously absent.

Melbourne is well supplied with omnibuses, cars, cabs and waggonettes, which are commodious and clean. Parliament, by special Act, authorised the construction of traction sub-surface cable tramways through the main streets of the city and the respective suburbs, most of which have been laid down by the Melbourne Tramways Trust, a body elected for that purpose by the city and suburban corporate councils.

There are inland towns in the colony which are deserving of mention, on account of their large and prosperous populations, as well as their substantial architectural characteristics. Ballarat, the second city in the colony, is situated one hundred miles from Melbourne. It has been well named the "Golden City." In the early days the gold-yielding powers of Ballarat were simply marvellous. No district in the world ever produced so much of the precious metal in so short a space of time. It has been stated that, in many instances, "claims" not more than eight feet square, and about the same depth, yielded from £10,000 to £12,000 each. At the Prince Regent mine, men made as much as £16,000 each by a few months' work. At one claim, a tubful of dirt yielded £3,325. The "Welcome Nugget," found in 1858 in the same neighbourhood, was sold for £10,500. Those days have gone, but Ballarat, as it is now, is still more wonderful than when gold was in very truth "more plentiful than blackberries." Anthony Trollope said of Ballarat, some fifteen years ago, that "in point of architectural excellence, and general civilised city comfort, it is certainly the metropolis of the Australian goldfields." Sturt Street, the principal thoroughfare, is a mile and a half long, two hundred feet wide, and has a fine row of trees in the centre. The principal buildings on either side are the city hall, post office, mechanics' institute, banks, theatre, hospital, and several large churches. The population is 40,000. The reservoirs, from which the water supply is obtained, have a storage capacity of 600,000,000 gallons. These works cost £300,000. Lake Wendouree now adds to the charming aspect of the city; hundreds of small yachts, miniature steamers, and rowing boats float on the lake, which is stocked with perch, trout, and carp. The botanical gardens, on the other side of the lake, are prettily laid out and well kept. Fine wheat and wool are grown in the neighbourhood of Ballarat, and the city has some repute for its iron manufactures, especially locomotives for the railways. The public buildings comprise a spacious hospital erected on high ground, orphan and benevolent asylums, lying-in hospital, refuge, public baths, mechanics' institute (with library of 12,000 volumes), free public library (with 13,000 volumes), extensive railway premises, 2 town halls, 3 theatres, and

POPULATION AND GROWTH.

about 40 churches. The educational establishments number 2 colleges, 4 grammar, 10 State, 3 denominational schools, and a Government school of mines. Three well conducted daily, and one weekly, newspapers are published. Over 84 miles of good streets have been constructed, and attractively planted with trees, and 164 miles of footpath are now made and channelled. There are 8 iron foundries, 13 breweries and distilleries, 4 flour mills, and 1 woollen mill; also, boot and other factories. Gold was first discovered at Ballarat in June, 1851. As the surface diggings became exhausted, it was found that richer deposits of the metal could be obtained at lower depths, to which fact is to be attributed the permanence of the progress of Ballarat. Returns from these goldfields show that the value of material employed is considerably over £300,000, the number of miners employed about 9,000, and the extent of auriferous ground now worked more than 856 square miles. The first juvenile exhibition in Victoria was held at Ballarat, and was very successful.

Sandhurst, or as it was originally termed, Bendigo, is a little over one hundred miles from Melbourne. It has about the same population as Ballarat, 40,000. It is the head quarters of a rich auriferous country, consisting principally of quartz ranges, which, from their almost inexhaustible character, will doubtless be a source of prosperity for years to come. There are about 1,000 quartz mining leases in the district, covering an area of over 18,750 acres, 160 mining plants being within the city, which is traversed by 100 miles of streets. The main street, named Pall Mall, abounds on one side with handsome brick and stone shops and stores, the opposite side being a reserve known as Rosalind Park. A substantial and ornamental building facing Pall Mall has just been erected by the Government, with ample provision for all the necessary public offices. There is a savings bank, hospital, benevolent asylum, mechanics' institute (with library of 6,800 volumes), branches of several banks, a fine theatre, and the town, masonic, temperance, and St. James' halls. There are three recreation reserves in the city, Rosalind Park, Weeroona Park and lake, and the botanical gardens, the latter beautifully laid out and planted with choice shrubs, and having a good collection of foreign animals and birds. There are eighty miles of trees planted in the streets, and the visual effect is very pleasing. The industries followed, besides gold mining, are represented by large iron foundries, railway carriage works, coach building factory, pottery, granite cutting and polishing, tanneries, brick and tile works, and cordial manufactories. Farming and wine-growing is largely pursued in the neighbourhood. Sandhurst has 19 churches; St. Paul's (Church of England) having an excellent peal of bells. Mining operations give employment to 6,500 miners, and 260 steam engines. The value of the mining plant is estimated at about £550,000, and the operations extend over 144 square miles of country. Three newspapers are published in the city. The Sandhurst School of Mines is well patronised. Instruction is given, not only in the various branches of science connected with mining operations, but also in many other subjects not necessarily connected with mining.

Geelong, which takes rank as fourth in Victorian cities, is picturesquely situated on the shores of Corio Bay. In the early days, having a rich back country, it for a long time promised to rival Melbourne, but a bar in the harbour proved an impediment to shipping, and the metropolitan city soon shot ahead of its temporary

POPULATION AND GROWTH.   31

rival. The population of the town is now estimated at 10,000. This is one of the oldest municipal townships of Victoria; it lies forty-five miles south-west of Melbourne. The town is well laid out, on ground sloping to the bay on the north side, and to the Barwon river on the south; and its streets abound with attractive shops, fine stores, and business premises. The principal buildings comprise the town hall, exhibition building, hospital, benevolent asylum, numerous churches, free public library, mechanics' institute (with library of 11,127 volumes), post office, branches of various banks, agencies of insurance companies, clock tower, grammar school, Geelong college, State schools, and the law courts. The botanic gardens, overlooking the bay, are extensive and well laid out. The public gardens and park are very fine. Corio Bay has four good jetties, alongside which ships of the largest tonnage can load and discharge. Geelong has the credit of establishing the first woollen mill in Victoria. The cloth is manufactured by hand loom and steam power. Four mills are in full operation. There are five wool brokers, a meat preserving company, one of the largest tanneries in the colony, and several excellent wool-scouring establishments. The increased facilities given for shipping wool direct to England, from the wharves, has led many growers and buyers to avail themselves of the saving thus effected. Extensive quarries of limestone are developed at the eastern boundary of the town, on the shores of Corio Bay. Two daily and two weekly newspapers are published.

Five of the suburbs of Melbourne are now cities, viz.: South Melbourne (formerly Emerald Hill), with a population of 36,000; Prahran, with a population of 34,000; Richmond, with a population of 31,000; Fitzroy, with a population of 30,300; and Collingwood, with a population of 28,500.

During the past three years there has been an extraordinary rise in the price of land in the city and suburbs, and the whole colony has shared in this evidence of prosperity. In 1886, as compared with the previous year, there was an increase of £525,627 in the annual value of urban rateable property, and of £302,018 in the country properties. The increase was much larger in 1887, but the figures are not yet available. During the years 1886-7 and 1887-8, Melbourne has been affected by a land boom of unprecedented dimensions as far as this colony is concerned. In the principal streets of some of the suburbs of Melbourne, land, which two years ago could have been bought for £50 a foot, is now selling at from £100 to £200 a foot. During the last twelve months land in some parts of Collins Street has advanced from £1,100 per foot to £1,500 per foot. In the best parts of Elizabeth Street the value of land jumped from £700 or £800 to £1,300 per foot. The old disused premises of the English, Scottish and Australian Chartered Bank in Elizabeth Street, sold by the bank for £33,000, were re-sold a few months afterwards for £45,000, and a short time afterwards changed hands again at the price of £61,000. All this happened within the past year, and many other similar instances could be quoted. Another remarkably profitable land transaction of recent times may be mentioned. In 1882, a man purchased a small allotment in Cavanagh Street, on the south bank of the Yarra, at £2 10s. per foot. He spent £2 15s. per foot in filling up the land and erecting a brick cottage on it; and a few months ago he found a purchaser at £70 a foot.

CHAPTER III.

METALLIC RESOURCES AND THEIR DEVELOPMENT.

VICTORIA owes much to its metallic resources as an initial element in its rapid development. To the attractions of the precious metal are due the vast influx of population which occurred between 1851 and 1857, and gold continues to be one of the leading exports. The gold mining industry comprises two principal descriptions, quartz and alluvial gold mining. In the first, veins and lodes, or reefs of quartz traversing the silurian rocks, and containing gold, are mined in much the same manner as other metalliferous lodes, and the quartz is crushed and the gold separated by means of mechanical appliances. The quartz is contained in the silurian rocks in an infinite variety of forms—as solid lodes, coinciding with the planes of the nearly vertical strata; as "saddle formations," resembling in cross-section a succession of inverted V's, thick at the apex, and thinning out in the limbs; as successions of blocks; as flat veins; and as assemblages of veins and bunches, following certain bonds of the silurian rocks. or traversing igneous dykes which intersect the latter. The gold occurs in the quartz in many forms as small specks, as strings and ragged pieces, occasionally attaining a large size, and, more rarely, as crystals or groups of crystals. The principal associated minerals are iron, copper, and arsenical pyrites, galena, and zinc blende; the iron pyrites frequently contain a large proportion of gold in mechanical combination.

Alluvial gold mining includes a number of different conditions, varying from "surfacing," where the gold is found in the thin soil and rubble, covering the surface of nearly exposed silurian rock to "deep lead" mining, where the concealed auriferous gravel deposits of ancient river beds are reached by means of sinking costly shafts through hundreds of feet of volcanic and sedimentary layers which overlie them. Under whatever conditions, however, it may be found, alluvial gold means *detrital* gold, or that which once contained in veins and reefs of quartz has been disintegrated and conveyed by geological action to various distances from the sites of those matrices.

Geological investigations tend to show that the gold-bearing reefs were formed in the silurian rocks of Victoria before the close of the palæozoic era, and that the upper portions of these rocks, with their contained quartz veins, have been planed off by denudation to the extent of thousands of feet in vertical height. All the alluvial or detrital gold deposits yet found in Victoria are red, older than the middle tertiary or pliocene epoch; many of them are post-tertiary or recent.

Some time before actual discoveries of gold were made, Sir Roderick Murchison predicted them on the strength of specimens of Australian rocks which had been sent to him. Station hands were also reported to have found pieces of gold, but the stories were hushed up, the squatters not desiring that their flocks and herds should be disturbed by an influx of gold seekers. The great discoveries in

METALLIC RESOURCES. 35

California, however, followed by those in New South Wales, caused systematic efforts to be made to achieve similar results in Victoria, and they were crowned with unexampled success. Between March and September, 1851, gold was found in large quantities at Clunes, Mount Alexander, Ballarat, Buninyong, the Pyrenees, and various other localities, which were speedily occupied by thousands of diggers.

James Esmond was the Victorian pioneer digger. He it was who found gold in payable quantities at Clunes on the 1st July, 1851. In 1848 he was driver of the mail coach between Buninyong and Horsham. For several years he had filled that monotonous position, when, attracted by the gold discoveries in California, he determined to try his fortune there. Meeting with no luck in California, he returned to Victoria, and occupied himself with bushman's work on a station in the Pyrenees. Presently a German geologist, named Dr. Bruhn, arrived on the scene, and showed to Esmond and his mate rich specimens of gold found in the neighbourhood. Esmond and his companion then, on the 1st July, 1851, entered on a prospecting tour. On reaching the banks of Deep Creek, a tributary of the Loddon, they were gladdened by the sight of glistening quartz. A little diligent fossicking there was rewarded by the unearthing of a few rich specimens of grain gold, or what appeared to be such. In order to make sure of the richness of the metal, Esmond determined to have the specimen tested by an assayer at Geelong. On arriving at that town the pureness of the gold was vouched for, and eager inquiries were made for the locality where the precious treasure could be found. Esmond declined to divulge his secret, and hastened to obtain the necessary implements and utensils for working the coveted field. It was the 6th of July before his digging expedition (the first in Victoria), which consisted of three men besides himself, was fully equipped. Before leaving Geelong, Esmond disclosed his destination to the assayer, who advised other parties fitting out for the Turon diggings to remain in the district, because of the probability of richer goldfields being shortly found close at hand. In the meantime another discovery was announced. A party of six men found sprinklings of gold in the bed of Anderson's Creek, a tributary of the Yarra, and only a few miles from Melbourne. Esmond's field attracted about thirty men, and produced satisfactory results until the end of August. It then became evident that the precious yellow grains were no longer to be found in the alluvial deposits. The men at Clunes were getting into severe straits because of the poorness of the shallow diggings when a visitor to the place brought the welcome news of fresh discoveries and encouraging prospects for diggers in the neighbourhood of Buninyong. Amongst the first to leave the Clunes diggings was Esmond, its original prospector. He joined a party of nine, who marched over the hills to the newly-discovered fields. Though remarkably successful as a digger, he was singularly unfortunate in his speculations. Subsequently, £1,000 was voted to him in reward for his discoveries. He also received a grant of a piece of land on the site of the first gold-field.

During the early days of the gold-fields, the diggers suffered a great deal from misgovernment. They were hunted by the police, and fired at if they could not produce their licenses when called upon, and it was a common thing to see a digger chained to a log, awaiting the adjudication of a magistrate, because he had not paid

METALLIC RESOURCES.

the monthly sum of thirty shillings; or because he did not happen to have the license in his pocket when called upon by a trooper to produce it. At the end of 1854 a large proportion of the diggers on Ballarat, exasperated by a failure of justice in a case in which one of their number had been murdered in a disreputable hotel, and, irritated by numerous tyrannical acts on the part of the police and the officials, took up arms, and entrenched themselves in a stockade, having some wild idea that they could overturn the Government. Mr. Peter Lalor, late Speaker of the Legislative Assembly of Victoria, was chosen leader. The diggers hoisted their standard—the Southern Cross—and five hundred of them took a solemn oath to fight to defend their rights and liberties. The Government forces consisted of police and soldiers. Captain Thomas, who was in charge of them, determined to take the insurgents by surprise, in preference to waiting for them to attack the camp. The attack was made just before daylight on the morning of Sunday, the 3rd December. Many of the disaffected diggers were not sleeping in the stockade, as they did not anticipate that the military would make any move before reinforcements arrived from Melbourne. The assault was brief but bloody. The stockade, which consisted chiefly of a barrier of ropes, slabs, and overturned casks, was penetrated in a few minutes, and the defenders, who fought vigorously for a time, were driven out into the shallow holes in the neighbourhood. Several volleys were fired on both sides, but most of the diggers who fell met their deaths in the shallow pits, where they were shot or bayonetted in the first heat of the conflict. The military force numbered 276 men. The loss of the latter also was considerable, including one officer, Captain Wise, of the 40th Regiment. Of the insurgents, 30 were killed on the spot, and a great many wounded. There were 125 prisoners taken in the stockade. The following account of the engagement was given by Raffaelo, an eyewitness:—

"I awoke Sunday morning. A discharge of musketry —then a round from a bugle—the command 'Forward'— and another discharge of musketry was sharply kept up by the red coats for a couple of minutes. The shots whizzed by my tent. 1 jumped out of my stretcher, and rushed to my chimney facing the stockade. The force within could not muster then above 150 diggers. The shepherds' holes inside the lower part of the stockade were turned into rifle pits. . . . . The dragoons from the south and the troopers from the north were trotting at full speed towards the stockade. Peter Lalor was on top of the first logged up hole within the stockade, and by his decided gestures pointed to the men to retire among the holes. He was shot down in his shoulder at this identical moment. It was a chance shot. I recollect it well, for the discharge of musketry from the military now mowed down all who had heads above the barricades. . . . . Those who suffered most were the pikemen, who stood their ground from the time the whole division had been posted on top, facing the Melbourne road from Ballarat, in double file under the slabs to stick the cavalry with their pikes. The old command, 'Charge' was distinctly heard, and the red coats ran with fixed bayonets to storm the stockade. A few cuts and kicks, a little pulling down, and the job was done; too quickly for their wonted ardour, for they actually thrust their bayonets through the bodies of the dead and wounded strewed about the ground. A wild hurrah burst out, and the 'Southern Cross' was torn down. Of the armed diggers some made

METALLIC RESOURCES.

off the best way they could, others surrendered themselves as prisoners, and were collected in groups and marched down the gully. . . . The red coats were now ordered to 'fall in,' their bloody work being over, and were marched off, dragging with them the 'Southern Cross.'"

When Mr. Lalor fell he was covered by his friends with slabs and escaped capture. In concealment his arm was amputated, and, though a large reward was offered for his apprehension, his hiding-place was never disclosed. The leading rioters were prosecuted by the Government, but the public sympathy was with them, and no jury could be found to convict. The riot, though it was deplored by the best friends of the men engaged in it, had the effect of directing attention to many evils suffered by the diggings population, and of eventually securing their remedy.

Most of the great goldfields were opened during the few years immediately following the first discovery, the prospecting population being then so great. Other new fields of less importance and extensions of old ones have since been opened from time to time, but no great discovery in shallow ground has been made for the last ten or twelve years. There are now leads being worked at from depths of from 400 feet to 500 feet. The position and depths of leads supposed to be auriferous are now usually first ascertained by means of boring, for which purpose diamond drills are extensively used. Shafts are then sunk through the superincumbent layers into the bedrock, drives are extended, and rises from the latter put up to the gravel, which, if payable, is then excavated and brought to the surface to be washed. Tens of thousands of pounds are frequently expended before the deep alluvial mines become remunerative, and sometimes after all failure is encountered; but successes have in the main counterbalanced the failures, and increasing experience tends to lessen the risk of the latter. There are still hundreds of miles in length of unworked leads, which are likely to reward future enterprise.

During the first five years of gold-digging little or no attention was paid to quartz-mining. The early modes of working quartz were rude, and for a long time the belief prevailed that the lodes were not likely to prove remunerative below a depth of 400 feet. from the surface. By degrees, however, it was found that in many reefs whose payable quartz had died out a short distance from the surface, other "makes" of auriferous stone were to be met with by sinking deeper, and confidence was restored as fresh discoveries were made at increasing depths in the quartz lodes of Stawell, Sandhurst, Clunes, and other mining centres. There are now many mines in which highly remunerative quartz is being obtained at depths varying from 1,000 feet to 2,500 feet.

The total yield of gold obtained in Victoria, from the first discovery to the end of 1886, has been 54,393,182 ounces, valued at £217,572,728; and the proportions of the total obtained respectively from quartz and from alluvial workings are about equal, though during the first ten or fifteen years the alluvial gold greatly exceeded in quantity that obtained from quartz. In future it may be expected that the yield from quartz will year by year progressively excel that from alluvial workings. Extensive and important as are the known quartz mines of Victoria, the total area occupied by them is insignificant compared with what are of probably similar character, which, although as yet untested, contain alluvial gold deposits, and these are a sure index of proximity to auriferous quartz. There is little cause to doubt that, as predicted by Mr. A. R. C. Selwyn, twenty years ago, the quartz lodes of Victoria will equal the tin mines of Cornwall as permanent fields for mining industry.

Dividends have been paid by Victorian gold-mining companies as follows:—

Quarter ended	Sept., 1886	£138,190
"	" Dec., 1886	130,265
"	" March, 1887	104,397
"	" June, 1887	95,267
	Total in twelve months	£468,119

The following table shows the estimated quantity of gold raised in Victoria from 1871 to 1886:—

	oz.		oz.
1871	1,355,477	1879	758,947
1872	1,282,521	1880	829,121
1873	1,241,205	1881	858,850
1874	1,155,972	1882	898,536
1875	1,095,787	1883	810,017
1876	963,760	1884	778,618
1877	809,653	1885	735,218
1878	775,272	1886	665,196

In his summary prefixed to the official report of the mining registrars for the quarter ended 31st December, 1887, Mr. C. W. Langtree, the Secretary of Mines, remarks:—"In my last summary I recorded an increase of 15,889 ounces for the quarter ended September, and now it is my pleasing duty to chronicle an increase for the December quarter, the figures being as follows:—

	oz.	dwt.	gr.
September quarter	160,102	6	7
December quarter	166,411	14	11
Increase	6,309	8	4."

The reports from the principal mining stations for the period are of an encouraging nature, and there is every indication that the present year (1888) will be more prosperous, as regards mining, than any of the last decade. The mining population of the colony for the final quarter of 1887 was estimated at 25,795, the number employed in quartz mining being 12,384, and 13,413 in alluvial mining. The area of auriferous ground actually worked is returned as a little over 314 square miles.

The subjoined table shows the value of minerals and metals other than gold produced in Victoria from 1851 to 1886:—

Name.	Estimated Value.		
	1851 to 1885.	Year 1886.	Total.
	£	£	£
Silver	72,041	5,284	77,325*
Tin	362,974	90	363,064
Copper and copper ore	105,559	1,922	107,481
Antimony	169,295	...	169,295
Lead	5.326	...	5,326
Iron	15.636	...	15,636
Coal	17,399	107	17,506†
Lignite	3,238	304	3,542
Kaolin	7,444	...	7,444
Flagging	65,294	1,883	67,177
Slates	2,732	1,536	4,268
Gypsum	7	...	7
Magnesite	12	...	12
Ores, mineral earthy clays, &c.	10,901	...	10,901
Diamonds	108	...	108
Sapphires, &c.	630	..	630
Total	838,596	11,126	849,722

* Of late years the silver raised has been extracted from gold in the process of refinement at the Melbourne branch of the Royal Mint.

† The quantity of coal raised was 13,153 tons.

Many attempts have been made in Victoria to mine for coal—notably at Cape Paterson—but the seams hitherto worked have been too thin to yield a profit. Thicker seams, however, have been discovered at the Moe and at

METALLIC RESOURCES. 43

Mirboo, in Gippsland, and it is considered not altogether improbable that valuable coal fields may yet be opened up in these localities. There is also some prospect of silver mining being profitably established at St. Arnaud. At present, however, the large silver yields are chiefly confined to New South Wales.

CHAPTER IV.

Agriculture.

THE agricultural resources of the colony, although only developed to a comparatively limited extent, have contributed in a marked degree to place Victoria in its present prosperous position, and the best guarantee for its future progress is to be found in the agricultural expansion, capable of resulting from its rich soil, genial climate, and various other advantages. It is only fifty-three years since the first white man settled upon Victorian soil, but a much shorter time has elapsed since the march of progress properly began with the inrush of population, soon after the discovery of, gold in 1851. The development of agriculture has a still more recent commencement, for, at the time of the gold diggings, the land was in the possession of Crown tenants, who leased it as sheep and cattle runs; and many years passed before the new colonists, attracted by the discovery of gold, could succeed in passing laws for the throwing open of the land to agricultural settlers. Up to the year 1860, land could only be obtained at auction, and it was difficult for men of small means to secure farms. Although more liberal land laws were passed after that date, it was not until 1869 that an Act was framed under which agricultural settlement was effectually encouraged.

AGRICULTURE. 45

Owing to the enterprise of the early colonists, first-class live stocks of different breeds had been imported from the first, so that, when the public lands where thrown open for selection in 1869, the colony was well supplied with trained farmers of local experience; stud herds of shorthorn, Hereford, Ayrshire, and Alderney cattle had been established, as well as studs of the best draught and thoroughbred horses, flocks of merino, Lincoln, and Leicester sheep, with well-bred representatives of other kinds of live stock. Under the Land Acts which preceded that of 1869, the greater portion of the best land in the coast districts had been alienated, many large estates used for grazing purposes having been formed, so that agricultural settlement, under the more liberal provisions of the new Act, had to extend mainly over the northern or inland portion of the colony. Settlements were rapidly formed in all parts of the northern plains, and wheat-growing, the most suitable industry for the pioneering stages of such districts, quickly assumed larger proportions. Three years after the Act came into force, viz., in 1873, the land under cultivation amounted to 965,000 acres, while ten years later the area had increased to 2,215,900 acres. The total extent of land under the wheat crop in 1873 was 350,000 acres, and in 1883 it was 1,104,400 acres. The land under cultivation in 1887 was 2,417,580 acres, and in the same year the land under wheat amounted to 1,052,685 acres.

The fertility of the Victorian soil is a well-established fact. Only a few years after the landing of the first settlers, potatoes grown in some portions of the western district won fame in older established parts of Australia, and other products were soon afterwards grown with equal success. At Belfast and Warrnambool the rich volcanic soil often gives a yield of from twelve to fifteen tons per acre of potatoes, and ten tons per acre is a common yield. The districts of Lancefield, Daylesford, Kyneton, Ballarat, and Gippsland contain land of the same kind, and all over the colony a large proportion of the soil is exceedingly fertile. Even in those parts of the colony where the yield of the crops is small, the defect is not so much in the soil as in the supply of moisture. There are in the inland northern portions of the colony, districts which do not enjoy such a liberal rainfall as others. In such localities the yield of the crops is generally comparatively light, but the soil is rich, a fact that is proved from the large yield obtained in a moist season. Having extensive areas of fertile soil in all parts of its territory, and consequently under different conditions of climate, the products of the colony are both abundant and varied.

The climate is of the most favourable kind. There is no winter in the English or American sense of the word. The time called winter is merely the season in which there is more rain and less heat than in summer. Very few Australians have ever seen snow. Upon the inland mountain ranges, and the elevated land in their vicinity, a little snow falls occasionally, but only sufficient to make the ground white for a few hours. The native trees are evergreen, not casting their leaves in the winter, although English trees and others indigenous to cold countries do. The winter is only a modified summer. Stock are neither housed nor fed in the winter.

The rich soil and warm genial climate combine to render the colony's productions abundant and varied. In the coast districts, where all kinds of cereals, leguminous and root crops are cultivated, the yields obtained from the unmanured land are all that could be desired. The average of the whole colony is always lower than the results obtained by farmers who understand their business. The system of farming carried on stands much in need of improvement. The majority of those upon the land have had no training as farmers, and the system, like that of all new countries, is not calculated to produce the best results. Farmers who understand their business, and give the land reasonable cultivation, obtain from 35 to 45 bushels of wheat, oats, and barley per acre in districts where the general average is not more than from 15 to 20 bushels per acre. Much heavier yields than those stated are frequently obtained, but from 35 to 45 bushels per acre are common when the land is well cultivated. With potatoes, mangolds, beets, and peas, the same difference is observed between the average obtained by a rough system of farming and upon land properly cultivated. About 5 tons of potatoes per acre is a payable crop, and from 12 to 15 tons per acre are frequently obtained. Hay, which is made from wheat or oats, yields from 2 tons to 4 tons per acre, and English grasses for pasture are successfully cultivated in all the coast districts. Maize is a crop which grows well in the more moist portions of the coast districts, and as much as 100 bushels per acre is frequently obtained. Owing to the defective system of farming, many of the crops for which the colony is suitable are much neglected, the tendency of settlers being to neglect rotation, and confine their attention to growing a single description of grain. Thus wheat-growing is carried on more extensively than most other departments of farming. All over the northern or inland districts wheat can be profitably produced, and in some sections other cereals do not thrive so well, and this fact also tends to swell the proportion of the colony's wheat production. The statistics of the harvest of 1887-8 show that the colony produced 13,328,765 bushels of wheat, 4,562,530 bushels of oats, 198,225 bushels of barley, 117,294 bushels of maize, 791,093 bushels peas, 161,088 tons of potatoes, 20,590 tons mangolds, 11,774 tons onions, 624,122 tons of hay, and 732,060 bushels of peas and beans. The wheat production of the colony is capable of great expansion, but there are more numerous opportunities and larger profits to be made by developing the various branches of husbandry which are partially neglected by the farmers.

The wheat grown in Victoria is the finest in the world. It always brings the highest price in the London market, fetching considerably more than English, Indian, American, or New Zealand wheat. The wheat crop is generally the first sown by the new settler, as it quickly returns a profit, and brings in resources to keep the farmer going until stock-raising, dairying, or other branches of industry are established. Many settlers have found continuous wheat-growing upon the rich virgin soil of the colony a profitable business; but the rule is that the best farmers, after a year or two, add the growing of other crops in rotation, and establish herds of cattle, flocks of sheep, breeding also horses and swine upon the farms.

Oats grow well in all the coast districts of the colony, and in the more moist of the inland districts. In the driest sections of the inland districts there is not moisture enough for the oat crop, but the area of the colony upon which oats cannot be cultivated is comparatively small. In the moist districts from 40 to 50 and up to 60 and 70 bushels per acre are obtained with good cultivation, and

AGRICULTURE.

the crop is successfully grown in rotation with wheat, barley, and roots.

As barley requires more moisture than wheat, there are dry districts inland from the coast ranges where it cannot be properly grown, but the area of its cultivation is more extensive than that of oats. It yields good returns all over the coast half of the colony, and upon about half of the inland area. English barley grows well, producing a fair malting sample and a good yield, the crop being a profitable one, although considerably neglected by the farmers, who generally give too much attention to wheat-growing. Those farmers who grow barley in rotation with oat, wheat, and root crops are generally the most successful.

The maize crop is one which is not understood by the majority of Victorian farmers. Although crops of 100 bushels per acre, or as heavy as in any part of America, are obtained, and those who engage in its cultivation make large profits, the majority of farmers pay no attention to the cultivation of this cereal. In America it is much more extensively cultivated even than wheat, maize being, in fact, the staple crop of the country. It is grown as a general crop in those states where only from 30 to 40 bushels per acre are obtained, and there are but few of the coast districts of Victoria where better yields would not be produced. The cultivation of maize, if attended to by the farmers, would be as profitable in Victoria as in many parts of America.

As in the case of maize, the cultivation of peas, beans, and vetches is much neglected by Victorian farmers. Peas have received some attention, and the result has been highly satisfactory. In the coast districts good yields are obtained, and the crop is profitable in more ways than one, for it has been found highly valuable in a system of rotation. Lands which had been impoverished by continuous grain-growing have been brought back to a state of fertility by sowing the pea crop, and in limited districts where the merits of the pea crop are understood it plays a leading part in the system of maintaining the productiveness of the soil. Beans, although growing fairly well in the moist district, are not extensively cultivated, and although vetches are found to do satisfactorily, their cultivation is at present limited. It is in the cultivation of many of these neglected crops that the agriculture of the colony could be greatly developed. The crude state of our farming system offers encouraging opportunities for an influx of farmers, whose skill would turn our various unused advantages to account.

The potato crop has been cultivated in most of the coast districts of the colony, and it yields a much higher return than cereals. Farms upon which potato growing is carried on usually command an exceptionally high value, a fact which bears the best testimony to the profitableness of the crop. Mangolds have also been successfully grown, very heavy crops being obtained, but, owing to the defective system of farming, the potato is the only root which has received much attention. Potatoes, being required for human food, find a ready market, and hence their comparatively extensive cultivation by the farmers; but as mangolds, beets, and carrots are required principally for feeding stock, they receive very little attention. Feeding stock is a system not properly understood in the colony. The rich pastures, and the absence of cold winters, enable farmers to keep their stock in the fields all the year round, and, at the same time, cause the business of feeding stock to be neglected.

Notwithstanding the richness of the pastures and the mildness of the winters, much could be done in the way of increasing the profitableness of stock-keeping by producing food, and the neglect of taking advantage of such an opportunity is one of the principal defects of our farming system. Those farmers who grow food for dairy cows, pigs, and other stock, find the system profitable, and they are generally more prosperous than their neighbours. Where heavy root crops can be grown, it is not the fault of the country if they are not cultivated. As the system of farming improves, the growing of mangolds and carrots may be expected to increase, and it is believed that the cultivation of beets for sugar-making will ere long become an important industry. Most of the onions used in the Australian colonies are grown in Victoria. The crop in the coast districts yields from ten to fifteen tons per acre, and the soil, which is never manured, shows no signs of exhaustion after more than twenty years' cultivation.

Hay, which is extensively grown in the colony, is made from oats or wheat, cut just before ripening. The yield is from two to four tons per acre, the last-named being the return obtained in the coast districts, and the former in the inland districts. In moist localities, or where irrigation is practised, lucerne is grown for hay, and it is one of the most profitable of crops. From four to six tons per acre are obtained, the crop yielding from four to six cuttings of about one ton each. In all of the coast districts, rye-grass, clover, cocksfoot, fog, foxtail, fesques, and other grasses are successfully cultivated, and it is the practice to lay down fields in pasture after they have been growing grain for a number of years. Very little manure is used in the colony, letting out the land in cultivated pasture being the most common means of maintaining fertility. In the northern or inland districts the rainfall is not sufficient to render the cultivation of English grasses profitable, but in those localities the growth of the natural grass is so rapid, and the quality of the pasture is so rich, no inconvenience is experienced from the absence of artificial grasses. After the cereal crop there is good pasture afforded by the self-sown grain, and in the second year the natural grass has established itself so well as to carry more stock than the unbroken pasture.

Hop culture has been established in the colony for some years, and there are extensive districts along the coast and near the mountain ranges specially well suited for the industry. Although hop growing was introduced at a comparatively recent date, and much had to be learned as to the cultivation of the plant and the treatment of the hops, the industry has already assumed an important position. The soil and climate are much better suited for hop growing than those of England or the eastern states of America, as shown in the higher yields obtained. From 20 to 25 cwt. per acre are frequently obtained from unmanured virgin soil, and about 10 cwt. per acre is yielded by yearling hops. California is the only country in the world that can show results equal to those of Victoria. Although such heavy crops are obtained, and the quality of the hops is excellent, only a few growers at present appear to understand the art of properly preparing the hops for market. Only a small quantity, therefore, is suitable for exportation to the London market; but, as the art of treating the hops becomes better understood, the industry will no doubt furnish a large quantity for export.

AGRICULTURE.

The tobacco crop is one which may be expected to increase as time passes. The soil and climate have been proved to be well suited for tobacco culture, and the cultivation of such a valuable crop may be expected to show development with the increase of population and the progress of the country. It will have been gathered from what has already been said that the climate resembles that of the south of Europe, and it follows that the various products of France, Spain, and Italy can be cultivated in the colony. This is not a matter of theory only, for experiments have already been tried which prove that the various rural industries of southern Europe can be introduced with an assurance of greater success than ever attended them in their native country. Fruits of all kinds—from apples, pears, plums, peaches, apricots, and cherries, to grapes, oranges, lemons, and olives—have been tried, and found to flourish in a manner which astonishes natives of the south of Europe. The mulberry grows luxuriantly, and the introduction of silk culture is only a matter of time. The only reason why the colony does not produce more fruits, olive oil, and silk is that it is too prosperous. Wages are so high that other industries involving less labour absorb the attention of the population. The state of California, however, the climate of which resembles that of Victoria, is teaching us that, by adopting machinery and labour-saving methods of management, many of the industries of southern Europe can be profitably carried on when the population is limited, and the rate of wages high. The attention of colonists has recently been attracted to the fact that in California fruit growing is developing marvellously on account of the system which is adopted of drying apples, apricots, prunes, raisins, and currants, and preserving fruit in cans, and efforts are already being made to introduce the same system into Victoria. Vines and fruit trees of all kinds grow well both in the coast and inland districts of the colony, and those colonists who are engaged in the cultivation of vineyards and orchards are generally even more prosperous than the farmers who grow grain.

There are many districts in Victoria which are admirably adapted to fruit growing. For years past Victoria has exported considerable quantities of dried and fresh fruits to neighbouring colonies, and within the last two years the beginning has been made of an export trade in fresh fruit with the United Kingdom, which is expected eventually to develop into large proportions. Shipments of Victorian apples, pears, and grapes to London have been well spoken of by the fruit merchants there, but much has yet to be learned in the matter of packing. It will, doubtless, be found in the future that refrigerating and other appliances will greatly aid the successful establishment of this trade. In the Old World it will, of course, be a great advantage to have fresh Australian fruit arriving at a time when fresh fruit of the same kind cannot be obtained in the northern hemisphere. When irrigation is more generously practised, large tracts of land, not good enough for agriculture, will be devoted to fruit growing. In Victoria land is nominally and really cheap. It gives such a good return upon the market value that it is considered by capitalists one of the best investments. During the last twenty years the Government have been offering the public lands at a low price to promote settlement. Land worth from £2 to £3 per acre could be had from the Government for £1 per acre, with from ten to twenty years to pay the purchase money.

AGRICULTURE.

This fact, together with the rough system of farming carried on, is sufficient to show that land could not rise to its natural value. Had an advanced system of farming been carried on, obtaining the best possible results from the soil, and if no land could be had without purchasing in the open market from holders who knew its worth, land values would have risen to their intrinsic worth. But land of the best quality could all along be obtained at the nominal rate of £1 per acre, with long terms, and the soil has not been developed to its full extent. At the present time purchasers get the advantages of these circumstances. They obtain land near markets and upon railway lines, at a cheap rate. In the inland dry districts, where land is rising in value owing to its productiveness having been tested, good land is sold at from £2 to £3 per acre. Farms with fencing and buildings upon them change hands at from £2 10s. to £4 10s. per acre. These may be taken as average prices. In positions specially convenient to large towns, first-class agricultural land is worth from £20 to £25 per acre, and land which is suitable for the potato crop fetches from £30 to £50 per acre, but these are exceptional values. It frequently happens that sheep farmers give from £2 to £3 per acre for unimproved grass land, to be used for grazing purposes alone, and the agriculturist can generally obtain a much larger return than the keeper of stock. It will be readily understood that the present value of land is low when compared with the returns obtainable from the soil, for the price is regulated by the circumstances of the country. Those circumstances which tend to keep down the price of land are the limited population, the quantity of Government land offered for the nominal sum of £1 per acre, with easy terms, and the absence of a system of high farming. When the Government lands are all taken up, and the growth of population increases, the demand bringing into existence also a system of high farming, land will command a much higher price than at present. The time is, therefore, a favourable one for obtaining cheap land. Farms are always to be had, as they change hands, and those who purchase within the next few years will not only make profits upon their agricultural operations, but at the same time gain advantage by the increasing value of the land.

The colony of Victoria is about 56,250,000 acres in extent. Of this area about 15,530,000 acres have been alienated to private owners. An area of about 7,584,000 acres is in process of alienation under a system of defined measurements, and after deducting roads, mining reserves and State forests there remains an area of about 30,000,000 acres available for settlement. Of the 30,000,000 acres available for settlement, 11,500,000 acres are what is known as the mallee country, which occupies the extreme north-western portion of the colony. The mallee country has been set apart for occupation under a system of leases from the Crown. The mallee in its present condition being insufficiently supplied with water, and covered more or less with a scrub of small trees and shrubs, is unsuitable for being taken up in farms of the ordinary size for agricultural purposes. The mallee is divided into two parts—viz., "the border" and the interior area. On the border allotments of various sizes up to 20,000 acres are let for a period of twenty years, and in the interior larger blocks are let for the same period. In the case of the border allotments the rent is fixed by regulation, and applications are granted without competition at a land board. The rents fixed for the interior blocks are 2d. per sheep and 1s. per head of cattle for the first five years, double those

AGRICULTURE.

amounts for the second five years, and 6d. per sheep and 3s. per head of cattle for the last ten years. At the end of the leases the land reverts to the Crown, and lessees are to be compensated for permanent improvements. It is expected that, at the expiration of the leases, the land, having been improved, will be suitable for occupation in smaller areas. The greater part of the mallee country has already been taken up, and occupiers have commenced to carry out improvements.

An area of about 20,000,000 acres of Crown lands, apart from the mallee, is now open for settlement under an Act of Parliament passed in 1885. This area is divided into pastoral lands and agricultural and grazing lands. The pastoral lands are surveyed in holdings capable of carrying from 1,000 to 4,000 sheep, and from 150 to 500 head of cattle. These pastoral holdings are leased for a term of fourteen years, the rent being 1s. per head for sheep, and 5s. per head for cattle, the carrying capacity of the holding to be determined upon a basis of not less than ten acres to a sheep. If there is more than one applicant for a holding, the block is put up to auction among the applicants, and given to the highest bidder. Lessees are required to destroy rabbits, wild dogs, kangaroos, and wallabies, and at the termination of the lease compensation is to be granted for such improvements as fences, wells, reservoirs and dams to the amount of 2s. 6d. per acre.

The agricultural and grazing lands, amounting to about 8,712,000 acres, are surveyed in blocks of not more than 1,000 acres each. These areas are leased for a term of fourteen years, the rents being fixed at not less than 2d. per acre or more than 4d. per acre, the valuation, according to quality, being made by officers of the Government. The allotments are surveyed, and shown numbered upon a plan. The applicant makes application for a given block, and if there are more than one application a land board decides which party is to obtain the land. The holder of one of these areas is not required to reside upon it, but he must destroy rabbits and other vermin, and fence his allotment within a period of three years. At the expiration of the lease compensation is granted for all such improvements as fences, wells, reservoirs, tanks and dams up to a limit of 10s. per acre. Upon the leasehold the occupier is allowed to cultivate for his own use, but not for market. Any male person eighteen years of age, who has not already selected land under any previous Land Act, is eligible to take up land under the existing law.

The occupier of one of these allotments can obtain the ownership of 320 acres upon easy terms. Any person who has not previously taken up land in the colony can select 320 acres of his leased land as a freehold. If an occupier selects a freehold, he must pay for it at the rate of 1s. per acre annually for six years. At the end of the six years he can either continue paying at the rate of 1s. per acre until a total amount of 20s. per acre has been paid, or he may pay the balance of 14s. per acre and obtain a Crown grant. The conditions are that the selector must reside upon his allotment, or within five miles of it, for six years, and within that period put on improvements to the value of £1 per acre. Persons who do not reside upon their selections must pay altogether £2 per acre for the freehold, and put on the £1 per acre improvements within three years. Under the existing law also grazing licenses are granted over auriferous lands and State forests.

A limited extent of Crown land is sold at auction annually, and special leases are granted for swamp lands, but the great bulk of the remaining State territory is dealt

AGRICULTURE. 59

with as pastoral lands and agricultural and grazing lands. It will be observed that the only means of obtaining the fee-simple of Government land in the colony is by taking up a 1,000-acre agricultural and grazing block, and selecting 320 acres out of it. In a few years the whole of the land will be taken up under the existing Act. The fact that the land is so quickly taken up is the best proof persons at a distance can have of the value of the land. Where there are large areas of free land awaiting settlement there must be adverse circumstances which render it unsuitable for profitable occupation. In the colony of Victoria land has always been eagerly sought after, and as it has been thrown open for occupation from time to time, under the different Land Acts, it has been quickly taken up. To the new-comer land ought to be worth as much, if not more, than to the existing settlers, for, while colonial farmers are rather prone to follow an old-time system of management, the new arrival brings with him improved methods, acquired amid the keener competition of older and more thickly-populated countries.

From what has already been said, it will be seen that the scope for agricultural development in Victoria is almost unlimited. With the exception of wheat growing, all branches of farming may be considered in their infancy. There is great room for improvement in the system of carrying on each branch of agriculture, and there are rural industries capable of almost unlimited extension, which have as yet made scarcely any progress. Of the total area of the colony—over 56,000,000 acres—not more than about 20,000,000 acres have been permanently occupied. The number of farm holdings is only 35,216, and not more than 2,417,552 acres are under cultivation. The cultivation amounts to only $2\frac{1}{2}$ acres for each person in the colony. Cultivation has of late years made satisfactory progress, and all the surroundings of the case show that the rate of development will be much more rapid in the future. The greatest increase has taken place in the production of wheat, a result which may be accounted for by the suitableness of the product for export, and the facilities offered by the crop in the way of giving a quick return to the occupiers of new country. Dairying, fruit growing, vine growing, hop culture, the cultivation of tobacco, and other lucrative branches of industry require some extra attention, and hence their progress has been less rapid. These latter industries are now receiving increased attention, and their progress opens up a very wide field for future development. For many years the special industries referred to have been kept back through having to depend upon the local markets. The American system of pushing exports of butter, cheese, hams and bacon, dried and canned fruits and vegetables out into the markets of the world has not been yet adopted, and hence prices have ruled low for what should have been our most valuable products. Now, however, steps are being taken to organise an export trade in the various products for which our soil and climate are specially favourable. A few fruit-canning factories have been established, and the increase of these will enable our orchards to be extended in every direction, supplying fruit to distant markets, and so on with the various rural industries which at present are subordinate to wheat growing. Those who are now engaging in agriculture will take part in the colony's new career of agricultural progress, and at the present time the colony offers special inducements to new-comers. It would be difficult to find a more promising field for the emigrant with capital, small means, or only his labour to depend upon. Wages are high, living is cheap, and capital commands a high rate of interest. The capitalist can find a profitable investment, be his resources extensive or limited, and the man who has no money can soon turn his labour into capital. Land being cheap, the freehold of a farm can easily be acquired, and the farmer carries on his industry upon rich soil in a mild genial climate, under the security of the British flag, and in a country where the rough pioneering system has given place to the comfort and conveniences, as well as the educational and social advantages, of civilised life.

CHAPTER V.

VINE CULTURE.

COMPARED with the old wine-producing countries of Europe, Australia as a sphere for the cultivation of the vine, is, of course, only in an infantile stage of development. But that nature has liberally endowed Victoria with all the conditions necessary for eminent success in the pursuit of this industry has already been proved beyond the shadow of a doubt. The verdict passed upon Victorian wines by experts of unchallenged reputation, combined with the increasing demand for them in the British market, renders the continuous expansion of our vineyards an absolute certainty, and the rate at which the remunerative production of wine in the colony progresses, resolves itself simply into a question of the wise and energetic application of capital, skill and enterprise. Twenty-eight years ago the space devoted to vine culture in Victoria amounted at most to 2,000 acres. Even at that early period in the existence of the colony, which was then barely nine years old, specimens of our vinous products, although as yet crudely manufactured, had found their way abroad, and received favourable notice. The generous recognition given them at the great International Exhibition held in London in 1862, and, subsequently, at similar industrial shows held at

VINE CULTURE. 63

Paris, Philadelphia, Amsterdam and Bordeaux, rekindled zeal in a pursuit which then had a tendency to languish. The local Government offered lands suitable for its operations on advantageous terms. Not a few men accustomed to very different occupations immediately plunged, in a speculative spirit, into wine-making, and large areas were soon taken up by companies, which, in some instances, failed to exercise needful caution in the selection of competent managers of the undertakings. Meanwhile, within a few years, 2,000 additional acres were planted. Melbourne journals stimulated the new-born enthusiasm by publishing, daily, reports of the wine "boom," and the proprietors of one newspaper awarded a handsome gold cup to the best appointed vineyard. As might be expected, this seemingly prosperous movement, being largely of mushroom growth, experienced a temporary collapse. A considerable number of the vineyards were established in districts unsuitable as regards temperature, and mistakes not less unfortunate were made in the choice of soil not adapted for the species of grape planted. Disappointment and failure, however, taught lessons of enduring value. The science of grape growing was more carefully studied, and thus a guarantee was afforded that the progress of the industry would be checked by fewer blunders in the future.

A few persevering vignerons, so far from being daunted by what had happened, were incited to renewed exertion, and at the Melbourne International Exhibition of 1881, samples of wine were displayed from the northern districts and around Melbourne, which marked a decided advance in the production, and from year to year since, this has been fully maintained. A considerable impulse was given to the industry by the offer of a trophy of solid silver, valued at £800, to be awarded by the late Emperor of Germany "to an exhibitor in one of the Australasian colonies, as an acknowledgment of the efforts in promoting art and industry, as shown by the high qualities of the goods manufactured by such exhibitor." The presentation of so substantial a premium on wine-producing merit, by so august a personage, proved to be a turning point in the history of viticulture in Victoria. Colonial wine, which had previously been looked upon with prejudice by people who had never tasted it, soon came to be spoken of at clubs, hotels, and domestic tables with respect. Before the lapse of many months, growers had the satisfaction of seeing the value of their properties rise in consequence. A spirit of friendly emulation among owners of vineyards to place a superior article on the market was created. Qualities of delicacy and bouquet, especially in light wines, which had before been neglected by makers of insufficient experience, began to receive proper attention. At the Indian and Colonial Exhibition connoisseurs were so favourably impressed with the samples of Victorian wines that depreciation of them suddenly ceased, and a growing inquiry has caused steady and increasing shipments of them to Europe ever since.

In 1886-7 the area under vines in the colony was estimated at upwards of 10,000 acres, and the quantity of wine produced amounted to 986,041 gallons. Mr. Hubert de Castella, one of the highest practical authorities in this description of manufacture in Australia, states that towards the close of the Exhibition of 1881, the proprietor of one of the vineyards on the Yarra Flats requested a representative of the well-known house of Arles-Dufour, of Paris, to take back to France with him specimens of his wines—then somewhat below their

VINE CULTURE.

present standard of excellence—and have them valued at Bordeaux. M. A. Lalande, to whom the wines were submitted, communicated the following gratifying report: "We have found the Nos. 1 and 2 (red wine, 1879, made from Cabernet-Sauvignon) very good, and we have given them a value of 1,000 francs per tonneau of 900 litres. We have found the No. 4 good (white Hermitage, 1879), and we have given it a value of 600 to 700 francs per tonneau." A verdict so impartial, pronounced by a judge possessed of unapproachable qualifications in his own department, permanently settles the question as to the position to which our wines are entitled. M. Lalande was told that the wines were of Australian growth, and was asked how their values compared with those of Bordeaux wines. The price of 1,000 francs per tonneau, which he fixed, was the price of the crus *bourgeois* superior of Margaux and St. Julien at two years old, just the age of the Australian wines he had tested. The price was also exactly the same as that of the third classified crus St. Emilion. The price of 700 francs for the Victorian white wines places them on a level with the fine white wines of the Gironde, "which, in the first crus, have a handsome pale yellow colour, much *finesse,* sometimes mellowness, and a very agreeable bouquet; they are worth, young, from 450 to 600 francs; old, they reach up to 700 francs per tonneau."

It may assist the reader in estimating the vast scope there is for development in viticulture here, to state that after the existing vineyard districts—still under very limited cultivation—have been fully utilised, they will constitute but tiny patches in comparison with the tracts of well-fitted and well-situated soil which await cultivation. The warm district of the Murray, of which Rutherglen is the centre, provides at present one-third of the vines grown in Victoria, although it only occupies a $\frac{1}{100}$th part of the total surface of the colony. But there is another enormous plain, composed of heavy red fertile soil, of great vine-growing capabilities, through which the Murray flows, and which is completely encircled by the River Ovens, and the Barambogie Ranges, the direct road from Melbourne to Sydney passing through the middle of it. The northern slopes in the centre of Victoria, from Stawell to Bendigo, a winding line of two hundred miles of mountains and gullies, all capable of producing splendid wines, are planted with scattered townships, which are destined to indefinite expansion in the future through the agency of the wine industry. Stawell, Ararat, Marong, Strathfieldsaye, Emu Creek, Castlemaine, Benalla, Sunbury, Essendon, the Yarra Flats, and the banks of the River Goulburn have already afforded convincing proof of rare productiveness in the manufacture of wines. But, after a population of millions has been prosperously established in these localities in the form of husbandry referred to, a stretch of land 500 miles long by 60 miles broad is in reserve, running from Cape Otway to the River Glenelg, and covering 16,000,000 acres, admirably adapted for viticulture, but as yet unknown to the grape.

It is justifiable to contrast the progress of wine-making in California with its much more tardy development in Victoria. We shall thus more fully realise our possibilities. The American state had only three years the start of the colony in its first great influx of immigration. At present the state and the colony have, as nearly as possible, a population of equal size. Both are situated in almost corresponding degrees of latitude north and south. Their rapid growth in the first instance was alike

VINE CULTURE. 67

due to extensive discoveries of gold. Yet viticulture—like all kinds of agriculture—has risen to dimensions in California, which, at the present rate of progress, will take Victoria twenty years to overtake. Against about 1,000,000 gallons of wine produced in Victoria in 1886-7, about 19,500,000 were produced in California, the returns of the state being about twenty times those of the colony. Nevertheless, so comparatively trifling is this greater quantity relatively to the requirements of the United States alone, that it will be long before California has any appreciable surplus to export to Europe. At the same time the European demand, when Victorian wines become more fully known, will be sufficient to overwhelm the vignerons of the colony with orders. The ravages of the phylloxera in France have diminished the wine crop of that country from 1,844,000,000 gallons in 1875 to 628,000,000 gallons in 1885. As the consumption of wine in Europe continually increases, the startling reduction which these figures show in the supply must be made up from some source, and no country has a more encouraging opportunity of taking part in providing for the deficiency than Australia. How very far Victorians still are from, even approximately, competing with the wine-producing countries of Europe for this purpose, is shown by the following table :—

WINE PRODUCED IN VARIOUS COUNTRIES, 1885.

	Gallons.		Gallons.
France	627,792,000	Spain (exports)	158,070,000
Italy	499,378,000	Holland	81,994,000
Austro-Hungary	207,328,000	United States	19,405,000

In addition to European markets, with a collective population of 250,000,000, India, Japan, and the Malay Peninsula—in which the people are only beginning to conform to the habits of Western civilisation—we have about 200,000,000 more among whom to introduce our products. This prospect ought to be animating enough to encourage even the most timid who command the requisite amount of knowledge and capital to enter a field of enterprise so boundless. An idea of the profit to be realised may be gathered from a statement by Mr. Hubert de Castella, himself a notably successful wine-grower:— "At Rutherglen, the district for us to judge by, there are five wine-growers, cultivating an average of 200 acres each, and 147 farmers an average of 12 acres each. Their wines cost them 6d. per gallon, or about that, and if they can sell them during the year following the vintage for 1s. 6d. per gallon, there is, on an average crop of 250 gallons per acre, a profit of over £12 per acre, which no other crop can give. A cultivation based upon such returns cannot but increase." The financial advantage to be reaped from buying from producers on the ground at the price of 1s. 6d. per gallon, and selling in bulk to consumers, may be estimated from the fact that it is impossible for a family in Melbourne to purchase a 2-gallon jar of the most common claret for ordinary table use at less than 9s., or 4s. 6d. per gallon. The price of two gallons, in bottles, at the vaults of wholesale dealers is 16s. to 25s., or at the rate of 8s. to 12s. 6d. per gallon. Such wine would readily fetch in London 30s. to 36s. per dozen, or 15s. to 18s. per gallon; and so satisfactory a price, it must be evident, would leave an ample margin for carriage to the Victorian port, freight to England, duties, dock dues, cellarage and warehouse expenses.

Closely connected with wine-growing is the preparation of raisins, a branch of grape culture not yet initiated on any scale in Victoria; indeed, the only vigneron from

VINE CULTURE. 69

whom the subject has received scientific attention in Australia is Mr. Hardy, of South Australia. In this form of grape culture, too, Victoria is immensely behind California, where, despite less favourable climatic conditions, the manufacture of raisins has already reached large dimensions. The successful cultivation of the raisin grape is only possible under uninterrupted sunshine, the absence of fog or rain during the period of ripening, a rich alluvial soil with moisture sufficient to keep the vine growing until the grapes begin to ripen, and immunity from spring frosts; but the areas in California having these indispensable conditions happen to be limited in number, and at considerable distances apart. On the other hand, the whole of the Goulburn Valley, with thousands of acres in other parts of Victoria, are exceptionally favoured in these conditions for the prosperous culture of the raisin grape. Ten years ago the raisin in California was unknown. In 1887, however, the production was close on 10,000 tons, and this supply will have to be six times as large before the demand of the Eastern States of the Union alone can be met. For this kind of fruit the Californian producer averages in the price he obtains in the dryer $2\frac{1}{2}$d. per lb., which gives to growers of raisins in the state a total of £200,000 per annum. In Fresno, San Bernardino, and Los Angelos, the prevailing extent of raisin vineyards is twenty acres. From these vineyards, with vines from four years old and upwards, the net annual profit per acre is from £15 to £50. In view of the small amount of labour required, it is not surprising that it should be the general opinion in California that raisin-growing is more profitable than any other branch of agriculture. Experience will, doubtless, prove the remark to be equally true as regards Victoria.

CHAPTER VI.

Dairy Produce.

DAIRY farming in Victoria is still in a crude stage of its development, but only requires increased scientific skill, enterprise and capital for its profitable expansion on a scale commensurate with its commercial importance. As a rule, farmers have yet to learn the necessity of bestowing special care, in the winter season, on the provision of shelter and feed for dairy cows, which, in most instances, at present receive only what food and shelter are supplied the year round in the open fields for cattle being fattened for market. That milking cows should yield so large a quantity of milk as they now do for domestic purposes, as well as for the manufacture of butter and cheese, in the absence of conditions immensely more conducive to the highest possible return of dairy products, is sufficient proof of the general mildness of the Victorian climate, and the abundance of grass obtainable in average agricultural and pastoral districts. In the countries of the Northern hemisphere, where the winters are usually long and severe, the same omission to provide adequate protection for dairy cows from frosty blasts and heavy snow storms would not only

DAIRY PRODUCE.

render dairy products impossible, but must be attended with fatal results to the animals themselves. Farmers are exceptionally to be met with in Victoria who not only place milking cows in sheds at night during winter, but are careful to feed them on straw or green fodder. But, despite the less considerate methods employed by the bulk of those who carry on dairy operations, the milk, butter and cheese annually produced in the colony is valued at a sum not far short of £3,000,000. The production in average years is equal to home demands, and leaves a considerable surplus for export to the neighbouring colonies. Neighbouring markets, however, are capable of absorbing the merest driblet of the vast amount of dairy produce which Victoria will be able to dispose of remuneratively when the industry is advanced far enough by the aid of the great mechanical processes so extensively worked in the United States, Canada, Denmark, Norway and elsewhere, to cheapen production and thus secure us a solid footing in foreign markets. Professor Arnold, the veteran scientific dairyman of America, writes:—" Dairy farming is the most appropriate and inviting for the recuperation of land exhausted by a succession of grain crops. It stops exhaustion, and brings good returns from the first. Forage crops grow well where grain crops pay poorly. Seeding down to grass gives time for air and water, heat and frost, to gradually unlock the tenacious compounds which hold the mineral elements of plants as with a firm grasp, and let them loose for the rootlets to feed upon, or to accumulate in the soil for future use. In this way a poor farm may be made to grow rich, and a rich one richer. These considerations ought to have weight in leading intelligent farmers to exchange the plough for the milk-pail."

In addition to the steady increase in the consumption of dairy produce, which cannot fail to go on *pari passu* with the growth of population, especially in the Australian colonies situated to the north of Victoria, we have awaiting what consignments of this description we can send them the markets of India, Japan, and the Malay Peninsula, to which butter, cheese, and eggs could be conveyed in a perfectly sound condition in properly regulated refrigerators. In addition to these countries, the United Kingdom—the greatest mart of all for our surplus produce—is ready to welcome at once the articles specified. A Canadian dairying expert remarks:—" All dairying countries are striving for a foothold in that market. Continental countries have an advantage over Canada and the United States because of their nearness to it. America has an advantage in her cheap lands, and in the greater aptitude of the people in devising new methods and making quick advance." But Victoria, when she rises to the occasion, will be found to have an advantage over both America and the European continent in supplying the dairy wants of England absolutely unassailable, notwithstanding our greater distance from the latter market. The cheap and easy accessibility of Melbourne from all parts of the colony, in contrast with the enormous stretches of country over which produce has to be conveyed at great cost, from the great west of the States and Canada to the seaboard, is a point in our favour not to be lightly esteemed. When it is remembered that there are five million acres in Victoria still available for pastoral, and eight million acres for agricultural and grazing uses, there can be no doubt but that plenty of good land is to be had in Victoria for a long time to come at a low price for dairy purposes. But our position at the extreme south

DAIRY PRODUCE. 73

of a vast continent in the Southern hemisphere places us under uniquely favourable conditions for supplying England, and enables us to defy both American and European competition. When it is summer with us, countries in the opposite hemisphere experience the rigours of winter, and dairy produce manufactured during spring and summer in the colony can reach Great Britain in time to supply the high winter market when the best fresh butter sells freely to retail consumers at 2s. 6d. to 3s. per lb. If the significance of this fact were duly pondered there would be an unprecedented accession of skill and capital to the dairying industry in Victoria as the most safe, enduring and remunerative in which it is possible to engage. The extent to which the mother country is dependent on foreign supplies of staple provisions is apparent from the following statistics from the Board of Trade returns for 1887. In that year the value of articles of food and drink imported into the United Kingdom from abroad, duty free, amounted to £116,930,359, or nearly one-third of the total imports of the country; butter and butterine being valued at £11,886,717; cheese, at £4,508,937; and eggs, at £3,080,561. It may be further stated that the bacon and hams imported were valued at £8,629,941. Towards these totals the United States contributed £1,850,000 in cheese and £6,350,000 in bacon and hams. From Canada the butter imported amounted to £121,250, and the cheese to £116,257. From Germany the eggs and butter received at British ports amounted to £1,370,144. From the Netherlands the butter received was valued at £1,776,000, and the butterine at £2,771,488. France forwarded £2,364,023 in butter, and £1,215,337 in eggs. From Denmark the butter and butterine imported into England in 1886 reached £2,196,476. From Belgium butter to the value of £215,529, and eggs amounting to £657,756 were imported in the same year.

Before, however, the goal of our hopes in doing a large dairy trade with the almost unlimited markets referred to is reached, the manufacture of butter and cheese must become more generally than at present distinct and separate industries from pasturing and milking cows. To produce these articles on a large scale requires factories and plant involving technical skill and outlay which only considerable farmers could be expected to command. In some cases the object is attained by the co-operation of those supplying milk, and in others by individual capitalists or joint-stock companies, exclusively devoted to dairy produce, as in the United States and Canada. In these countries the separate factory system secures the extraction of a larger proportion of cheese and butter from the milk by economical methods than is possible in such dairies as are commonly attached to farms. Owners of factories buy the milk from the farmers of the district, the attention of the former being concentrated on the production of the commodities manufactured of a uniformly high quality. The advantages of the co-operative system in cheese-making, which has risen to very large proportions in America, naturally led to its application to the making of butter, and the initial effort in the latter direction was what is called the *creamery*. Under this arrangement the milk is taken to the factory to be set and skimmed, and the cream churned into butter. This system has been greatly stimulated by the introduction, in recent years, of the De Laval cream separator, which is gradually coming into use in Australia. The main forms of co-operative dairying at present are, the cheese factory for making cheese only; the butter factory, for making butter

DAIRY PRODUCE.

only from milk; the creamery, for making butter from cream, which has been collected from surrounding farms; the centrifugal factory, or the separation of the cream by the De Laval machine and the churning of that product into butter; and the skim-cheese factory, where partial or complete creaming for butter is adopted, and the skim-milk is manufactured into skim-cheese. These particulars are given to show the limitless scope that there is for expansion in dairying operations in the colony, and the rich rewards awaiting those possessed of the requisite knowledge, means and energy to turn out dairy produce suitable for English, Indian, and other markets.

CHAPTER VII.

WOOL.

VICTORIA has hitherto ranked below New South Wales, as regards the quantity of wool she produces, but the amount of her annual clip exceeds that of every other colony of Australasia; and if only the visitations of drought and market depression—the two arch-enemies of squatters—do not occur with inconvenient frequency, her progress as a grower of wool is certain to be materially greater in the future than it has been in the past. The quantity of wool produced in Victoria in 1886 is estimated at 57,439,634 lb., the value being £2,791,923. This aggregate represents the excess of exports over imports during the year, to which is added the quantity and value of wool used in the woollen mills of the colony. In the twelve months preceding, the quantity produced, reckoned on a similar basis, was 53,390,100 lb., valued at £2,960,890. On a rough average the yield of New South Wales has been two-thirds greater than in Victoria, while the latter colony produces over a fourth more than Queensland, and nearly a fifth more than South Australia. The production of Western Australia, despite its enormous area, is barely equal to that of Tasmania, although in both these colonies it is at present comparatively insignificant.

It will be observed from the figures given above that, although the quantity produced in 1885 was considerably less than in 1886, the value realised in the former year was much higher than in the latter. This seeming anomaly is due to the heavy fall in price which was experienced in 1886, when the declared value of wool before leaving the colony, according to the Customs' returns of exports, was only 11¼d. as against 1s. 1⅜d. in 1885, 1s. 5¾d. in 1884, and 1s. 3⅜d. in 1883. Indeed, the depreciation of wool in Victoria during 1886 was equal to a total of £436,000 in comparison with a similar quantity in 1885, and of £1,453,000 as compared with a similar quantity in 1884. The price just stated for 1886 is the average for all descriptions of wool included in the one total in that year, so that it is possible that a variation in the quality may, to a certain extent, account for the difference in the declared value. But the cause last mentioned operated in an inappreciable degree in weakening market values, compared with the glut of supplies with which Victorian sellers, in 1886, especially, had to contend. "Good to superior wool," the produce of Victoria, which in 1880 yielded 23½d., and in 1884 22½d., only realised 18d. in 1886. The year 1887, as distinguished from the immediately previous twelve months, was one of the most uneventful periods in the annals of the wool trade. The variations in price in that period, though in no instance wide, showed a declining tendency on the whole, but not on the serious scale of 1886. The chief characteristic of Victoria, as a wool-growing colony, is the unrivalled adaptation of its climate and pasture lands for the production of the merino wool. It is not, of course, maintained that the merino sheep cannot be grown in other Australasian colonies. All that is affirmed is that the description of merino fleece produced in Victoria is universally recognised in European markets as bearing away the palm; and the conditions of pastoral settlement in the colony strongly favour the culture of wool on a large scale by the class of moderate grazing farmers, who are fast elbowing out the squatters.

South Australia at first began sheep farming on small freeholds, and developed the squatter system on leasehold from the State, which still exists. Victoria, on the contrary, from the outset and for many years afterwards, was the paradise of leviathan squatters, with scarcely any freehold runs for the first twenty years or more; but a wholesome change is passing over the country. Instead of now, as a rule, meeting with flocks of considerable magnitude wandering over vast areas, it is the happy tendency of Victoria to become a colony of small grazing farmers. It cannot be expected that pastoralists of limited means can afford to pay fancy prices for high-class rams to improve the breed of their flocks, nor command means for the erection of expensive machinery to prepare their wool for market; but, occupying as they do, limited areas, they are much more favourably situated than the squatting class are to advance the quality of the native grasses, to employ irrigation methods, and thus to obtain, by extra care, a higher percentage of lambs and raise to a higher standard existing breeds. In this way they secure an augmented market value for their wool. Besides, throughout the colony, by the extended distribution of law-abiding and industrious families, which the breaking-up of large runs into small leasehold and freehold farms effects, the profitable culture of the larger kind of sheep having long wool is promoted—the latter branch of pastoral industry being favoured by the demands of increasing urban populations. By the steady operation of the changes which have just been indicated, moreover, squatters of the great territorial type are driven further north into regions surrounded by conditions conducive to the successful cultivation of merino wool.

When the fall in prices became pronounced in 1885-6, a scare was created on the alleged ground that the Australian trade in wool would be hopelessly ruined by over-production resulting from the competition of the River Plate and the United States; but an analysis of the facts has proved the apprehensions which had been entertained to be utterly unfounded. It may be an open question whether there is not some risk of the demand for inferior qualities of wool being sooner or later overtaken, but these are not the qualities for which Victoria is most celebrated; and it is noteworthy that the values of the finest qualities which prevail in the colony were not, after all, very seriously affected during the late period of depression.

The fear is expressed in some quarters that the greater cheapness of land and its superior carrying capacity in the countries bordering on the River Plate, confer on pastoralists in that part of the world advantages which must eventually dislodge Australia from her position of supremacy in producing wool of the finest texture. But the excessive fluctuations which take place in the supplies of South American wool, from climatic causes, constitute a drawback which operates even more injuriously than the occasionally protracted droughts do which visit Australia. In Monte Video the pasture is not deemed by skilled graziers to be suited for sheep; and it often happens in that state that after some progress has been made in the culture of flocks and prosperity seems assured, an epidemic breaks out and sweeps them off wholesale. Moreover, the scourge is aggravated by the absence of all law for its prevention, the result being that the infliction is liable to spread through the carelessness of neighbouring selectors. In the Argentine Confederation the process of "refining" is found to be necessary for the purpose of rendering grazing land fit for depasturing stock. In its natural condition the grass is tall, and so intermingled with scrub as to be very rank, and only suited to support animals of a low grade or actually wild. Before superior breeds of sheep can be sustained upon it, portions of this coarse vegetation must be burned off; and it is not before three years have elapsed—during which the burning process has been repeated several times—that the grass becomes as fine as that of an English meadow, which is estimated to carry about two sheep to the acre. Competent observers, travellers in South America, have remarked that one Australian sheep yields as much profit as two sheep do in Buenos Ayres. In that country flocks of about 2,000 have to be shepherded and yarded every night owing to the prevalence of heavy dews, and, unless they are protected from these on dry ground, they are in danger of dying off in large numbers from foot rot. Under these circumstances all ground for alarm lest South America should favourably compete with Australia in the better kinds of wool disappears. In second-class descriptions Victoria might perhaps be closely approached, but in fine long-combing wool the colony has no superior, while at the same time it is free from many fatal influences to which the countries alluded to are exposed. On patches of land at once limited and widely apart, in that region, it cannot be denied that fine qualities of sheep can be grown; but the reverse is the case as regards the Argentine provinces in the main.

It is not surprising that the quality of merino wool produced in Victoria should for the most part out-distance that grown in other countries, when the exceptional conjunction of circumstances favouring its production is considered. Unquestionably the excellent climate—suited for pasture lands—and the skill of her flock-masters are important factors in bringing about the result. But the sources from which the original Victorian merino flocks were derived, show their pedigree to be of the very highest character. It is fortunate for the present wool-growers of the colony that the pioneers of the pastoral interest in the older colonies of Australia had a sufficient combination of skill and capital to secure the finest breeds of sheep. The first persons to introduce sheep into Victoria were the Messrs. Henty, who were also the first settlers in the colony, and the merino sheep which they brought with them were of the premier class. The flock was formed in England towards the end of the last century, with pure merinos obtained from the flock of the king, George III. Mr. Henty's sheep took the first prize wherever he exhibited them in England, till he was ultimately debarred from competition, owing to the unchallenged superiority of his sheep, compared with those of any other flock in Great Britain. It was a portion of this flock that was first shipped to Western Australia in 1829 in charge of Mr. Henty's two sons; but as the sheep did not thrive there they were transferred to Tasmania, where the sons were joined by their father with the rest of the flock. Disappointed in reference to a promised grant of land from the Government of the latter colony, the Hentys sailed for the mainland of Australia, and took up their residence at Portland Bay, Victoria. Through bad management and neglect the flock itself has been entirely dispersed and lost, but sheep from it have been used in many of the most famous studs of the colony.

The Van Diemen's Land Company formed a second source from which the early colonists of Victoria obtained merino sheep. Opportunities of buying were afforded at the annual sales of the company, which imported all descriptions of stock into Tasmania, and in a single year they expended £30,000 in the purchase of merino sheep from the best flocks in Germany. A number of private individuals in those days imported Saxon merinos, and of their produce a fair share of the best specimens found their way into the infant colony of Port Phillip. Captain MacArthur in 1797 imported a few merinos from the Cape of Good Hope—the first merino sheep imported into Australia. The flock thus established was crossed by a few rams bought by Captain MacArthur from the stud of George III. Since that time the flock has remained without any addition of foreign blood. In distinction from the flock of the Hentys, that of MacArthur has been preserved, having passed into the ownership of the Hon. William Campbell, of Victoria, and it has materially contributed to sustain the high pastoral standing of the colony. In a few studs, French sheep from the Rambouillet flock have been made use of, and, in one or two other cases, American merinos from Vermont have been introduced; but the pedigree prized above all others in Victoria is the Saxon merino, and the pure descendants of that breed still take the very highest rank.

The merino is the sheep invariably bred on large pastoral properties, situated in the warmer and drier portions of the colony. On the other hand, in parts where the rainfall is above the average, the long-wool is the sheep favoured by farmers. Of long-woolled breeds the Lincoln is that most approved. In districts heavily grassed and moist, near the southern coast, there are many flocks of long-wools kept, some of the Lincolns comparing favourably with any of the breed imported from England, in weight, lustre, quality of fleece, and size of animal. Leicesters, which received attention for a time, are now being merged in Lincoln flocks. The Romney Marsh sheep are reared in a few cold and wet localities, but their numbers are trifling in comparison with merinos and Lincolns. One or two small flocks of Cotswolds and Southdowns are bred in Victoria; but, although they cannot be regarded as unprofitable, they have never won the unqualified admiration of Victorian flockmasters.

As irrigation districts multiply, and it is fully ascertained, by experiment, in what way fodder for sheep can be grown and stored against a bad season, it may be hoped that multitudes of flocks, which now perish from drought and its consequences, will be preserved. There are indications that the question, as to how provision can best be made for the contingency referred to, is beginning seriously to occupy the attention of sheep-owners. Of course, it is farmers having facilities for growing the required crops on an adequate scale that will prove most successful in this enterprise. Indeed, already fully one-half of the wool, and the greater part of the fat sheep sold in the Melbourne market, come from agriculturists who are small flock-owners. The quality of their wool is steadily improving, and their consignments are eagerly sought after by stock-agents. Lamb breeding for the markets will probably be monopolised, as time goes on, by the small sheep-owners. Sheep-farming is a profitable industry in all countries, but it is in Victoria that sheep give the highest return for the capital expended. Land that can support a sheep per acre in its natural state can be bought at from £3 to £3 10s. per acre, and where sheep grazing is united with agriculture, the former can hardly fail to prosper. The greater proportion of the lands suitable for sheep-husbandry are now alienated from the Crown, but land for this purpose can be purchased from private owners in almost any part of the country at reasonable prices.

It will greatly assist a visitor to Melbourne in forming an idea of the magnitude of the wool trade in Victoria, to inspect the enormous warehouses erected expressly to accommodate the storage of wool in the interval between its arrival and its shipment. The magnificent structure of Messrs. Goldsbrough & Co., which is of immense length, has five flats, and a storage capacity of 64,212 tons measurement, the collective area of the floors being 5·61 acres. It is built of solid bluestone, with walls that appear impregnable. The cost of the land and buildings was £167,000. The New Zealand Loan and Mercantile Agency Company occupy exceedingly handsome warehouses built for a similar object, at a cost, exclusive of the land, of £95,000. The Australian Mortgage and Agency Company have an extensive wool warehouse, also in the heart of Melbourne, capable of storing large quantities of wool. The premises of Messrs. Monckton D. Synnot Brothers are also of considerable dimensions. But the wool trade of Victoria, great as it is, is

WOOL. 85

destined yet to attain much more gigantic proportions. A scheme was proposed when the European wool market was so heavily depressed in 1886, to form a Victorian syndicate for the purpose of taking over the woollen mills belonging to the Government in Japan, and erecting others in that country and in China, to supply the markets of the world with woollen cloth made from Australian wool. The cheapness, ingenuity and extended hours of Japanese and Chinese labour formed a prominent consideration in connection with the scheme, and, had it been carried out, as was confidently anticipated at the period mentioned, there is little doubt that a revolution would have been effected, not only in woollen, but gradually in cotton manufactures. But before that scheme had reached maturity, the prices of the raw material rose in the English market, and the squatters who had promised to co-operate decided to withdraw, the undertaking collapsing in consequence. At the same time, it is by no means improbable that when the evil day next temporarily overtakes the pastoral interest in Victoria, the scheme may be revived. Meanwhile, it is reported that the Japanese themselves are moving in the matter, and have sent over representatives to cultivate wool in Victoria for their market.

CHAPTER VIII.

COMMERCE AND FINANCE.

IMPORTS AND EXPORTS.—The latest period for which the imports and exports of the colony have been published is 1886, in which year the total declared value of imports amounted to £18,530,575, and of exports to £11,795,321. The excess of imports over exports is thus shown to be £6,735,254, the total of the external trade in both departments being £30,325,896. The value of imports was higher in 1886 than in 1885 by £485,971, or by about three per cent.; but, as compared with the year last named, the value of exports experienced a falling-off, amounting to £3,756,437. Of this decrease about nine-tenths were spread over thirty-nine articles of home produce or manufacture; but, on the other hand, there was an increase of £172,306 spread over sixteen articles of home produce. The decrease in the exports of 1886, as compared with those of 1885, was most prominent in four articles, viz., gold specie, £2,345,344; sheep, £324,91·; wheat, £242,277; and wool, £121,879. The suspension of the frozen meat shipments to England, and the low prices of wheat and wool, account for the export decline in three of these commodities, and the large diminution in the amount of gold specie is satisfactorily explained. In the twelve months now under notice there was an unusually large amount of money

COMMERCE AND FINANCE.

remitted by bank drafts and bills from the parent country to Victoria for investment, and the gold was retained in Victoria, and drawn against by remittances in the manner described, a simple exchange operation found to be more profitable by the banks than sending the specie to Europe. The imports of 1886, judged by their values, were higher than in any other year since the colony was founded, with the exception of 1884 and 1882. The great expansion of population, however, which took place in 1886 is apparent from the fact that, notwithstanding the exceptionally high total of imports, the value of these per head of the population was lower than in any of the last fourteen years, except 1879 and 1880, and also lower than in most previous years. The colony being under the somewhat sudden necessity of supplying the wants of an unusually large number of new comers with agricultural and pastoral produce, had, as might naturally be expected, a proportionately smaller surplus left for export.

The following table from Hayter's *Year Book*, shows the position of Victoria among the colonies as regards the total value of imports and exports in 1885, and in the eleven years 1875 to 1885.

Order in 1885.	Order in a Series of Years.
1. New South Wales.	1. New South Wales.
2. Victoria.	2. Victoria.
3. New Zealand.	3. New Zealand.
4. Queensland.	4. South Australia.
5. South Australia.	5. Queensland.
6. Tasmania.	6. Tasmania.
7. Western Australia.	7. Western Australia.

In comparing the trade of New South Wales with that of Victoria, it should be noted that the import and export returns of the latter include each year a considerable value in wool brought to Melbourne from the neighbouring colonies as a convenient port of shipment. In proof of the marvellous strides made by the collective external trade of Australasia, it may be stated that it now exceeds that of the United Kingdom at the time of the Queen's accession. During the years 1837-40 the total external trade of the parent country averaged £115,000,000 per annum, against £117,000,000, which was the average united trade of the Australasian colonies during the years 1883-85, the latest period to which the Government statist has brought down the calculation. It need hardly be remarked that the trade which the colonies carry on with each other is included in this total, as well as with countries outside the Australasian colonies, the result being that the same merchandise is necessarily reckoned in the returns of more than one colony in all cases in which intercolonial trade is carried on. The aggregate intercolonial trade of the Australasian colonies in 1885, according to the returns of each, was £42,601,533; and it is generally believed that if only intercolonial tariff barriers were entirely removed by the establishment of a federal Government and federal Parliament, combined with a Customs union, and uniform duties on imports from the outside world, an impulse would be given to intercolonial trade by which it would soon be increased fourfold. The total value of the external trade of the Australasian colonies, taken as a whole, while less than that of the United Kingdom and India, is much larger than the external trade of any other possession. In an estimate which has been published of "Inter-British Imperial trade," *i.e.*, mutual trade between the United Kingdom and her possessions, and that carried on by the various sections of the empire with each other, Victoria stands nearly equal to New South Wales, is fifty per cent. in

COMMERCE AND FINANCE. 89

advance of Canada, and beats the record of every other British possession, except India. The value of imports per head in Victoria is nearly twice as large, and the value of exports per head is more than twice as large, as in the United Kingdom.

Mr. Hayter affirms that, " omitting the small colonies of Malta and the Falkland Islands, the value per head of Victorian imports and exports is greater than that of the imports and exports of any British colony outside of Australasia, except the Straits Settlements. The external commerce of Victoria is much larger than that of Denmark, Greece, Portugal, or Roumania," and it may be added that, taken per head of the population, it is nearly as large as that of Belgium, which has almost six times the number of inhabitants contained in Victoria. The proportion which the Victorian productions exported bear to the whole, ranges from seventy-seven to about eighty-two per cent.

The principal imports comprise wool, chiefly from New South Wales, for transhipment, sheep and horned cattle overland, hardware, woollen, cotton and silk fabrics, railway plant, galvanised iron, gold and silver bullion and specie, coal, timber, tea, tobacco, leather, boots and shoes, sugar (raw and refined), spirits, fruit, preserved fish, haberdashery, drugs and chemicals, machinery, books and stationery, and pianofortes. The leading articles exported are wool, woollen and cotton fabrics, gold, books and stationery, hats and caps, hosiery, preserved fish, flour, raw and refined sugar, spirits, leather, hay and chaff, paper, timber, oils, coal, chinaware, earthenware and glass, iron, railway plant and various manufactures of metal, horned cattle, and ordnance stores. It will be readily observed that a considerable portion of the export trade consists of commodities received from abroad and re-exported. At the same time an analysis of the Customs' returns shows Victoria to rank above every other colony of Australasia in the value of the indigenous produce exported except New South Wales, whose much greater extent of territory enables the latter to raise a very large quantity of wool and other pastoral produce, which is only partially counterbalanced by the extensive quantities of grain and gold produced in Victoria. Yet the difference in favour of New South Wales in 1885 was only half a million sterling. In 1886, as regards value, nearly half the Victorian imports were from the United Kingdom, and more than half the exports were consigned to that country. In the same year the imports from the United Kingdom amounted to £8,851,801, and the exports to that destination £6,566,118. The imports from New South Wales reached £4,350,871, and the exports to that colony £2,624,713.

SHIPPING.—The rapid expansion of Victorian commerce is apparent in the circumstance that, although the population of the colony increased by less than one-half during the sixteen years ending 1886, the tonnage of vessels entered and cleared at the close, as compared with the commencement of that interval, increased nearly threefold. It is also noteworthy that while the population in the six years ending 1886 increased only 19 per cent., the tonnage in 1886 as compared with 1880 increased 55 per cent. Statistics show that the tonnage of vessels trading to Victoria exceeds that to any British possession outside Australasia except the United Kingdom, Gibraltar, Malta, India, Ceylon, the Straits Settlements, Kong Kong, and Canada. The aggregate tonnage in 1886, both inwards and outwards, exceeded considerably that of any previous year. The four latest years for which the figures are accessible when this compendium went to press are compared in the following table:—

Year.	Tonnage of Vessels Entered. Tons.	Tonnage of Vessels Cleared. Tons.
1883	1,464,752	1,499,579
1884	1,569,162	1,582,425
1885	1,631,266	1,628,892
1886	1,848,058	1,887,329

Of the total tonnage in 1886, 52 per cent. was colonial, 35 per cent. British, and 13 per cent. foreign.

BANKS OF ISSUE.—There are eleven banks of issue in Victoria, which had within the colony 419 branches or agencies in 1886.

The position of the banks as regards liabilities, assets, capital and profits, according to the sworn returns for the last quarter of 1881, 1886 and 1887, was as follows:—

	Dec., 1881.	Dec., 1886.	Dec., 1887.
LIABILITIES.	£	£	£
Notes in circulation	1,359,495	1,399,208	1,461,068
Bills in circulation	60,198	92,981	67,699
Balances due to other banks	330,414	354,328	448,431
Deposits not bearing interest	7,425,356	7,239,681	9,161,963
Deposits bearing interest	13,726,554	23,999,721	23,154,399
Total	22,902,017	33,085,989	44,293,560
ASSETS.			
Coined gold, silver, and other metals	2,695,474	4,565,990	6,512,573
Gold and silver in bullion and bars	313,017	366,950	326,146
Landed property	901,253	1,222,260	1,388,616
Notes and bills on other banks	144,034	151,089	178,933
Balances due from other banks	336,611	239,556	292,994
Debts due to the banks	22,783,420	34,625,144	38,034,062
Total	27,173,809	41,170,989	46,733,324

	Dec., 1881.	Dec., 1886.	Dec., 1887.
CAPITAL AND PROFITS.	£	£	£
Capital stock paid up	9,143,122	9,568,418	10,100,742
Average rate per annum of last dividend declared	9·981 %	12·141 %	£12 1s. 10½d. %
Amount of last dividend declared	456,300	580,875	611,371
Amount of reserved profits after declaring dividend	2,694,329	4,669,116	5,218,947

A comparison of the returns for the three periods specified shows a marked expansion of banking business. The advances in 1886 exceeded the deposits by 1½ millions in 1881, while the excess of advances over deposits as compared with 1885 was 3½ millions, and in 1887 the excess over 1886 was about the same amount. The capital of the banks was larger in 1887 than at any former period, while the reserve was higher at the last-named period than in 1881 by about 2¾ millions sterling, and higher than in 1886 by more than half a million. The average rate of dividend in 1887 was higher than in 1881, the rate varying in the case of different banks from 7 to 17½ per cent. The rate of discount on bills at two to three months, which in 1881 ranged from 5 to 8 per cent., ruled in 1886 and 1887 at from 6 to 9 per cent.; and for overdrafts the average bank rate was 9 per cent. But these rates have not been generally maintained in 1888, in consequence of the exceptional influx of capital from Europe during the past 12 months. The rates of interest allowed on moneys deposited with the leading Victorian banks for a period of 12 months have ruled at about 6 per cent. per annum. In 1887 there was a reaction from the cause which has been mentioned, the deposit rate having fallen from 6 to 4 per cent, at which latter figure it remained in June, 1888.

SAVINGS BANKS.—The number of savings banks connected with the Post Office in 1886 was 264, the number of depositors 78,328, with a total of £1,266,957 remaining on deposit. In the same year there were 15 general savings banks having 111,031 depositors, having £2,322,959 remaining on deposit. The aggregate represents 279 savings banks, 189,359 depositors with a total of £3,589,916 remaining on deposit, being an average of £18 19s. 2d. to each depositor. It appears that Melbourne and its suburbs contain 62½ per cent. of the total depositors in the Victorian savings banks, and 61 per cent. of the total deposits is held in the metropolis and its immediate neighbourhood. It is no inconsiderable evidence of the thrift prevailing in the wage-earning portion of the community that in the 15 years between 1872 and 1886 the number of depositors in savings banks has increased two and a half times. For several years previous to 1880 the amount standing to the credit of the depositors had been almost stationary, but in subsequent years a steady increase has taken place, and in 1886 it had risen to upwards of 3½ millions, or more than twice the amount six years previously. In 1886, as compared with 1885, there was an increase of 18,665 in the number of depositors of sums under £100, depositors of £100 and upwards having increased only by 678. The savings banks have always paid interest at 4 per cent., which is the highest rate they are permitted by statute to give. The number of male depositors in the year last referred to was 61,550 against 49,481 females. The moneys deposited with the Post Office savings banks are placed to the credit of a trust fund, part of which is invested in Government debentures and stock, and part deposited with the banks. The general savings banks' deposits are invested in loans on mortgage or in Government debentures and stock, or are deposited with the banks. In proportion to population the number of depositors is greatest in Victoria of all the Australasian colonies.

BUILDING SOCIETIES.—Another proof that the spirit of thrift prevails in the colony is the multitude of building societies which exist and apparently flourish. At the close of 1886 the number was 60, and since that date many more have been added, all of them being established within the last 25 years. These institutions are utilised by the less opulent of the community for two purposes. A large section of those practically interested in them obtain advances by which they are enabled to buy land and erect houses in a country which offers special facilities to small freeholders, the loans being repaid by instalments at short intervals until the ground and dwellings are completely redeemed; others deposit their earnings with these institutions for fixed periods at 5 to 6½ per cent. Against a total of 19,907 investing members in these sixty societies there were in the year under notice 16,250 borrowers, chiefly on security of houses and land of the class indicated above. The amount of paid-up capital supplied by the proprietaries, as a whole, was £2,502,799, and the amount to the credit of depositors and current accounts was £2,910,791. Advances made during the 12 months, subject to periodical repayments by fixed instalments, reached £2,358,728—an amount, it will be noticed, which is considerably under the total of the paid-up proprietors' capital on the one hand, and still more below the aggregate amount of deposits and current balances to credit on the other. Subscriptions on investing shares received during the year amounted to £318,044, and the repayments of loans in the same period was £1,526,220. The value of landed property held by the societies in fee simple was £391,698, a portion of which, it is fair to assume, came into their hands owing to the stoppage of periodical repayments. The collective amount of bank overdraft to the debit of the sixty institutions was £262,191, and the aggregate working expenses for the year was £62,369, the latter item being little over £1,000 for the cost of management for each society.

PUBLIC REVENUE. — The amount of Government revenue collected during the 12 months 1887-8, was £7,607,753, which shows an increase of £873,928 on the total figures for the year immediately preceding, and £751,047 above the budget estimate for the former period. There was an increase of nearly £288,142 in the income from railways, and the Customs Department collected upwards of £220,689 more than in the year 1886-7. The annual public income above specified is the largest as yet received in the history of the colony.

OPENINGS FOR INVESTMENT OF CAPITAL FROM ABROAD. —It may be affirmed, without the smallest exaggeration, that no country in the world at present affords scope so encouraging for the investment of European capital, with or without the residence of investors. There are many existing branches of industry and commerce which admit of indefinite expansion, and it is absolutely certain that the Centennial International Exhibition will materially contribute to multiply channels for Victorian trade, and lead to an exchange of products with countries which have hitherto participated but little in the commerce of the colony. Since the Exhibition of 1880-1, Germany has established a great and growing trade with this part of the world. Austria and her Teutonic neighbour, which have both been accustomed to purchase merino and long-combed wool in the London market, are expected, ere long, to found agencies in Melbourne for buying these products and sending them direct to German and Austrian ports. In exchange for the rice, tea, and sauces received from India, the colony gradually develops a profitable export business in remounts for the Indian cavalry service, and many other productions will yet be transmitted from this side to the Indian peninsula.

Enough has been stated in another chapter in reference to the favourable attitude of the markets of England and France towards Victorian wines to stimulate their manufacture on a vastly more extended scale than has yet been attempted. Private and joint stock capital, prudently invested in the establishment of vineyards, cannot fail to produce, in a few years, handsome returns. The culture, also, of table grapes for export to Europe is a department of horticulture which has, as yet, hardly come into existence, notwithstanding that it contains the latent germs of thousands of fortunes. The aid of science may require to be called in for the purpose of teaching viticulturists the art of effectively packing grapes, which is brought to perfection in Southern Spain; and more precise attention will be necessary in regulating temperature in the cool chambers of the steamers plying between Australia and Europe, where a cargo of a nature so perishable is concerned. But these questions of detail are sure to be satisfactorily arranged in due time. Not less hopeful prospects await the expansion of the export of hard fruit, raisins, oranges and olives. Our consignments of these varieties to Europe will arrive at a season of the year when the home market is bare of supplies. The trial shipments already made of apples and pears to the United Kingdom from New South Wales and Tasmania, as well

COMMERCE AND FINANCE.   97

as from Victoria, demonstrate that, with increased skill and care, the difficulties surrounding the problem of how to land such perishable produce in sound condition at English ports will entirely disappear.

Reference has been made to the unlimited demand which exists in Great Britain for butter and cheese, which Victoria is in so excellent a position for manufacturing and supplying advantageously. Here, too, is a comparatively unexplored mine of wealth, the extent of which cannot be fully known until the butter and cheese factories largely in operation in the United States and Canada are widely introduced in Victoria.

It is to be regretted that the tentative efforts previously made to export dead meat to Europe have not proved financially successful; but the day is not far distant when attempts will be renewed, under remunerative conditions, to export preserved as well as dead meat.

Although gold-mining is an industry too firmly established in the colony ever to be neglected, its precarious character precludes advice being given in favour of the indiscriminate investment of British capital in Victorian mines; but eminently satisfactory results will assuredly reward the enterprise of those having means and energy sufficient to undertake the development of our fisheries on an adequate scale for colonial supply, employing their own nets and boats, conveying the fish to a central market under their own control, and adopting the Roosen process for preserving without salting the fish until they can be profitably disposed of.

The extent to which British capital is already safely and remuneratively invested in land in Victoria abundantly proves the confidence felt in the rapid growth of its population, its manufactures, its agriculture, its pastoral resources, and its commerce. Existing land mortgage companies and private agents are respectively employed as mediums by British investors. But the absorbing power of the colony can be fully realised only by a lengthened residence in it. It must always be borne in mind that Melbourne is the most wealthy, enterprising and populous city in the whole of Australasia, and from its splendid climate and central maritime position on the southern coast, is destined not only to become immeasurably larger as the capital of Victoria, but, sooner or later, also, as the commercial capital of a federated Australia. It is this double consideration which explains the growing value of land in Melbourne and its beautiful suburbs. Interest on money lent upon sound land mortgage at $5\frac{1}{2}$ to $7\frac{1}{2}$ per cent. can readily be obtained. The following table shows the number and amount of mortgages on land in 1886, and it is unquestionable that the figures have grown much larger since:—

Consideration.	Number of Transactions.	Amount.
		£ s. d.
Under £100	917	50,577 16 6
From £100 to £150	2,549	396,821 3 1
„ £250 to £500	2,301	782,075 10 7
„ £500 to £1,000	1,852	1,142,933 4 9
„ £1,000 to £5,000	1,682	3,058,999 7 9
„ £5,000 and upwards	377	6,114,656 7 0
Unspecified	1,291	—.
Total	10,969	£11,546,063 9 8

The number of releases of mortgages of similar amounts in the same period represent 6,840 transactions, and a total of £5,031,488. The number of transactions in mortgages given upon sheep, cattle, horses and pigs was 1,123, and the amount £392,753 13s. 10d.

CHAPTER IX.

DEVELOPMENT OF MANUFACTURES.

AS a manufacturing country Victoria occupies a superior position to that of any other colony of the Australasian group, a circumstance which is in a large measure ascribed by many to her protective tariff. The grinding of corn was naturally one of the earliest industries established in the colony, and it has increased with the growth of agriculture. The number of mills in operation in the colony at the end of last year was 120. Of these 112 employed steam power, and the remainder water power. The number of hands employed was 743, and the tons of flour made 163,015. The machinery and plant in use were valued at £240,400, and the buildings at £163,810. The brewing industry has always been a prosperous one in the colony. The number of breweries in operation last year was 72. The beer made amounted to 16,088,462 gallons, the machinery and plant in use were valued at £140,170, and the buildings at £212,135. The quantity of beer imported, after deducting exports, was 1,135,253 gallons. These numbers give a total consumption of 17,223,697 gallons, or an average of $17\frac{1}{2}$ gallons per head. There were in operation, in 1887, 226 brickyards and potteries, with 58 machines worked by steam power, and 103 by horses, the number of hands employed being 2,271. The bricks made were valued at £349,960, the pottery at £45,400, the machinery and plant at £185,369, and the buildings at £133,995. The number of tanneries, fellmongeries, and wool-washing establishments was 140, employing 1,546 hands, with steam engines of 773 horse power. The number of hides and skins tanned was 1,753,473; the number of skins stripped of wool, 1,923,009, and other wool washed, 10,497,303 lbs.; the machinery and plant were valued at £106,420, and the buildings at £134,008. There were 8 woollen mills in 1887, employing steam engines of 866 horse power. The quantity of wool used was 1,651,458 lbs.; and the goods manufactured were 995,026 yards of tweed, cloth, flannel, &c., 2,507 pairs of blankets, and 228 shawls. The hands employed were 387 males, and 317 females. The machinery and plant were valued at £146,036, and the buildings at £63,300. The number of soap and candle works in 1887 was 34, employing 408 hands. The soap made amounted to 130,609 cwt., and the candles to 46,714 cwt.; the machinery and plant were valued at £73,358, and the buildings at £36,720. The tobacco manufactories numbered 11, employing 460 males and 196 females. The tobacco manufactured amounted to 1,181,283 lbs.; the snuff to 2,365 lbs.; and the number of cigars to 7,293,460. The machinery and plant were valued at £31,225, and the buildings at £20,515. The number of distilleries was 8, employing 56 hands. The spirits made amounted to 239,444 gallons; the machinery and plant were valued at £29,050, and the buildings at £24,075. There were manufactories, works, &c., exclusive of those already named, to the number of 2,151, employing 32,545 males, and 5,807 females, with machinery and plant valued at £3,834,829, and buildings valued at £2,267,434. There were 155 stone quarries in work, employing 1,458 hands. The stone raised was valued at £167,210; the machinery and plant at £52,119, and the buildings at £8,705.

The manufacturing establishments of all kinds, respecting which returns are obtained, are named in the following table, and their numbers are given for 1880-81 and 1886-7. For the former, which was the census year, are also given the approximate values of the materials used, and articles produced, and for the latter the number of hands employed, and the approximate value of lands, buildings, machinery, and plant. The establishments are for the most part of an extensive character, the only exception being in cases where the existence of industries of an unusual or interesting nature might seem to call for notice. No attempt is made to enumerate mere shops, although some manufacturing industry may be carried on thereat. Were this done, the "manufactories" in the colony might be multiplied to an almost indefinite extent. It is customary to note all establishments where machinery, worked by steam, gas, water, wind, or horse power is used. It is believed that a different system prevails in some of the neighbouring colonies, and that particulars of many establishments which, in Victoria, would not be considered worthy of notice, find place in their returns.

MANUFACTORIES, WORKS, &c., 1881 AND 1887.

Description of Manufactory, Works, &c.	1880-81			1886-7		
	Number of Establishments.	Approximate Value of— Materials used.	Approximate Value of— Articles produced.	Number of Establishments.	Hands employed.	Approximate Value of Machinery, Plant, Lands, and Buildings.
		£	£			£
BOOKS AND STATIONERY.						
Account-book manufactories, manufacturing stationers	7	62,386	100,057	7	723	183,315
Printing establishments (including paper-bag manufactories)	89	202,475	569,797	145	3,555	696,450
MUSICAL INSTRUMENTS.						
Organ-building establishments	2	3,500	8,050	4	31	6,700
Pianoforte manufactories	5	1,700	4,150	3	13	2,690
CARVING FIGURES, &c.						
Statuary works	...	...	...	2	5	2,050
DESIGNS, MEDALS AND DIES.						
Die-sinkers, engravers, medallists, trade-mark makers	6	3,350	9,200	6	70	15,260
Indiarubber stamp manufactories	2	350	1,700	...	...	...
Type foundry	1	...	...	...	...	...
PHILOSOPHICAL INSTRUMENTS, &c.						
Electric-lighting apparatus manufactory	...	...	...	1	...	...

MANUFACTURES.

Philosophical instrument manufactories	1	...	...	3	14	4,090
SURGICAL INSTRUMENTS.						
Surgical instrument, truss—manufactories	6	2,400	5,600	4	16	7,310
ARMS, AMMUNITION, &c.						
Blasting powder, dynamite, &c.—manufactories	3	9,964	16,737	7	75	37,570
Fuze manufactory	1	...	...	1	...	...
Shot manufactories	...	...	...	2	5	5,550
MACHINES, TOOLS AND IMPLEMENTS.						
Agricultural implement manufactories	54	91,659	202,535	63	948	143,937
Boiler and pipe-covering manufactories	...	...	...	1	...	...
Cutlery, tool—manufactories	3	800	2,400	5	23	8,960
Domestic implement manufactories (including bellows, churn, washing machine, &c., makers)	2	...	...	9	64	24,165
Iron foundries and engineering establishments (including brass-founders and pattern-makers)	147	329,395	723,919	154	5,699	1,013,866
Nail manufactories	...	...	...	3	22	8,000
Pattern-makers	...	...	...	5	15	6,225
Sheet-iron and tin works	61	143,000	247,299	49	776	137,740
CARRIAGES AND HARNESS.						
Carriage lamp manufactories	3	900	2,950	2	15	3,250
Coach, waggon, &c.—manufactories	132	99,415	212,615	183	2,407	290,135
Perambulator manufactories	3	1,750	5,000	3	13	4,310
Saddle, harness—manufactories	47	35,792	81,130	53	496	90,970
Saddle-tree, &c., manufactories	4	2,400	6,860	4	21	4,075
Whip manufactories	3	940	2,950	2	12	1,365

Manufactories, Works, &c., 1881 and 1887.—(Continued.)

Description of Manufactory, Works, &c.	1880-81.			1886-7.		
	Number of Establishments.	Approximate Value of—		Number of Establishments.	Hands employed.	Approximate Value of Machinery, Plant, Lands and Buildings.
		Materials used.	Articles produced.			
		£	£			£
Ships and Boats.						
Ship, boat—builders	10	3,570	14,614	9	162	8,690
Ships' wheels, blocks, &c.—manufactories	3	505	1,100	1	...	...
Floating-dock	1	...	...			
Graving-docks	3	...	...	8	164	437,668
Patent slips	2	...	...			
Houses, Buildings, &c.						
Architectural modelling works	11	3,584	8,900	12	56	12,985
Patent ceiling ventilator manufactories	2	250	1,600			
Enamelled mantelpiece manufactories	...	...	...	3	29	3,620
Lime works	21	6,560	17,216	37	340	14,082
Roof-covering composition manufactories	2	944	2,180	...	...	...
Venetian blind manufactories	12	5,500	11,750	11	98	16,875
Furniture.						
Bedding, flock, and upholstery manufactories	15	13,350	26,880	22	200	49,860
Cabinet works (including billiard table makers	63	131,000	258,188	68	1,211	182,627
Bedstead manufactory	...	...	...	1	...	...
Earth-closet manufactory	1	...	...	3	24	6,550
Iron-safe manufactories	2	670	970	2	15	3,600

MANUFACTURES. 105

Looking-glass manufactures	2	400	1,300	3	25	4,950
Picture-frame makers, &c.	13	5,627	11,550	6	26	10,580
Wood-carving and turnery works	10	4,965	10,300	16	69	14,925
CHEMICALS.						
Chemical works	6	25,160	43,600	10	151	55,630
Dye works	6	1,130	7,150	8	65	15,310
Essential oil manufactories	4	1,825	3,900	8	52	8,320
Ink, blacking, blue, washing-powder, &c.—manufactories	12	37,280	58,560	7	185	38,570
Ironfounders—charcoal manufactory	...	...	...	1	...	...
Japanner	1	...	...	1	...	...
Paint, varnish—manufactories	...	...	...	1	18	11,550
Printing ink manufactories	...	...	...	3	34	3,432
Salt works	8	4,882	10,810	8		
TEXTILE FABRICS.						
Woollen mills	10	89,412	168,710	8	704	217,104
DRESS.						
Boot manufactories	105	355,418	686,922	92	3,574	189,028
Clothing factories	63	370,181	761,401	72	3,656	307,041
Fur manufactories	3	4,300	6,000	4	24	6,350
Hat, cap—manufactories	22	34,753	66,264	16	457	60,780
Hosiery manufactories	...	...	...	3	21	2,080
Oilskin, waterproof-clothing manufactories	5	900	5,700	5	56	6,110
Umbrella and parasol manufacturers	9	13,180	24,825	7	121	13,695
Wig manufactory	1	...	...	...	...	...

Manufactories, Works, &c., 1881 and 1887.—(Continued.)

Description of Manufactory, Works, &c.	1880-81.			1886-7.		
	Number of Establishments.	Approximate Value of— Materials used.	Approximate Value of— Articles produced.	Number of Establishments.	Hands employed.	Approximate Value of Machinery, Plant, Lands, and Buildings.
		£	£			£
Fibrous Materials.						
Rope, twine, mat, bag, sack—manufactories	18	66,975	102,280	12	278	87,957
Sail, tent, tarpaulin—manufactories	12	28,860	47,250	9	56	18,345
Animal Food.						
Butterine factory	1	...	...	1	...	...
Cheese factories	28	17,733	31,586	16	57	18,505
Meat-curing establishments	16	192,150	258,790	25	314	52,919
Vegetable Food.						
Arrowroot, maizena, oatmeal, starch—manufactories	5	5,620	8,000	1	...	...
Biscuit manufactories	13	106,110	181,840	6	588	70,500
Confectionery works	8	61,600	88,800	12	419	71,630
Flour mills	144	1,397,099	1,637,351	120	743	472,069
Jam, pickle, vinegar, sauce—manufactories	25	84,430	132,170	23	406	79,905
Macaroni works	2	125	230	1	...	...
Drinks and Stimulants.						
Aërated waters, gingerbeer, liqueur, &c.—works	114	91,849	196,810	141	954	238,525
Breweries	81	442,885	780,501	72	1,037	550,901
Coffee, chicory, cocoa, mustard, spice—works	12	235,355	322,786	13	282	148,940

MANUFACTURES.

Distilleries	6	26,368	44,500	8	56	105,535
Malthouses	14	67,635	98,000	16	107	81,270
Sugar, treacle—refineries	1	...	...	2	165	207,000
Tobacco, cigars, snuff—manufactories	16	126,450	199,320	11	656	80,940

ANIMAL MATTERS.

Boiling-down, tallow-rendering—establishments	15	28,303	77,000	16	72	22,735
Bone mills and bone manure manufactories	15	50,225	70,845	13	92	33,355
Brush manufactories	8	15,700	27,800	8	154	18,120
Comb manufactory	1	...	...	...	...	...
Catgut manufactories	2	800	2,000	1	...	...
Curled hair manufactories	3	1,700	2,565	1	...	...
Glue, oil—manufactories	7	8,200	12,700	4	22	5,650
Leather belting (machinery) manufactory	...	...	...	1	...	...
Morocco, fancy leather—manufactories	3	2,480	4,400	4	20	2,440
Portmanteau, trunk—manufactories	7	5,680	9,520	5	22	8,410
Soap, candle—works	38	288,340	450,924	34	408	151,054
Tanneries, fellmongeries, and wool-washing establishments	151	1,008,531	1,406,274	140	1,546	319,983

VEGETABLE MATTERS.

Bark mills	8	17,000	25,650	3	18	4,180
Basket-making works	9	1,670	4,560	12	65	10,745
Broom manufactories	2	6,200	13,000	1	...	...
Chaff-cutting, corn-crushing—works	165	357,232	516,623	203	867	225,467
Cooperage works	24	17,829	35,243	24	134	29,535
Cork manufactories	2	2,100	3,100	1	...	...
Fancy-box, hat-box—manufactories	5	3,080	6,745	7	112	17,165
Paper manufactories	3	24,300	47,370	2	201	97,800
Saw mills, moulding, joinery, &c.—works	174	552,463	973,127	267	4,618	679,711

MANUFACTORIES, WORKS, &c., 1881 AND 1887.—(Continued.)

Description of Manufactory, Works, &c.	1880-81			1886-7		
	Number of Establishments.	Approximate Value of— Materials used.	Approximate Value of— Articles produced.	Number of Establishments.	Hands employed.	Approximate Value of Machinery, Plant, Lands and Buildings.
		£	£			£
COAL AND LIGHTING.						
Gasworks	19	97,392	226,116	21	572	1,598,822
Electric-light works	...	...	...	1	...	...
STONE, CLAY, EARTHENWARE, AND GLASS.						
Artificial stone manufactory	...	...	...	1	...	...
Asbestos works	...	...	...	1	...	...
Brickyards and potteries	165	...	137,834	226	2,271	548,026
Cement tile works	...	...	...	1	...	...
Filter manufactories	1	...	...	3	12	3,180
Glass manufactories—works	9	12,705	41,150	5	113	22,350
Stone-breaking, asphalte, tar-pavement—works	9	10,640	27,783	...	...	...
Stone and marble sawing, polishing—works	43	50,583	104,614	45	624	84,922
WATER.						
Ice manufactories	2	2,000	7,000	3	40	33,800
GOLD, SILVER, AND PRECIOUS STONES.						
Goldsmiths, jewellers, and electro-platers (manufacturing)	28	62,020	109,050	18	305	99,375
Royal mint	1	...	...	1	...	...

MANUFACTURES.

METALS OTHER THAN GOLD AND SILVER.

Bell foundry	...	1	...	...	...	...
Brass and copper foundries	...	...	...	...	17	371	85,507
Lead, pewter, and zinc—works	...	5	17,850	28,800	2	16	21,000
Pyrites works	...	1	...	...	1	...	...
Smelting works	...	7	32,896	48,610	4	94	32,750
Wire-working establishments	...	10	3,650	9,800	7	57	13,140
Total where only one return was received for each of certain descriptions	...	257,910	400,080	...	274	173,910
Total ...	2,468	7,997,745	13,370,836	2,770	45,773	11,028,158

CHAPTER X.

SOCIAL STATISTICS: BIRTH, MARRIAGE AND DEATH RATES. EDUCATION, SCHOOLS AND UNIVERSITY. RAILWAYS, TELEGRAPH AND POST OFFICES. RELIGIOUS STATISTICS. COST OF LIVING. VICTORIA AS A FIELD FOR SETTLEMENT.

VITAL STATISTICS.—Marriages in Victoria numbered 7,737 in 1886, or 342 more than in the previous year. In 1887 there was a further numerical advance to 7,768. The annual marriage rate was thus 7·84 per 1,000 of the population in the former year and 7·62 in the latter. The proportion which the number of marriages bears to the total population is generally called the marriage rate. This for many years has been declining in Victoria, for, whilst in the three years prior to 1863 it was above 8 per 1,000 of both sexes and all ages, from 1863 to 1865 it was between 7 and 8, and between 1868 and 1878 it was between 6 and 7 per 1,000. It reached its lowest point, 5·90 per 1,000, in 1879, and then gradually revived, and in 1886 mounted to 7·84, the highest rate which has prevailed during the last twenty-four years.

Births in 1886 numbered 30,824, or 31·23 per 1,000 of the population, and in 1887, 33,043 or 32·40. During

STATISTICS. 111

the twenty years ending 1883, the number of births in Victoria had remained almost stationary; but in 1884 a marked increase took place, which was more than sustained in 1885, 1886, and 1887, the number of births in the latter being the highest ever recorded. In proportion to population, however, the births decreased steadily for a number of years.

The death rate in 1886 was 15·17 per 1,000 of the population. Over a period of twenty-six years the deaths of males per 1,000 of the same sex living exceeded by $2\frac{1}{8}$ the deaths of females per 1,000 of that sex living. It has been held by high authority that in countries in which the climate is healthy, hygiene properly attended to, and the population in a normal condition as regards age, the ordinary mortality incident to population would probably cause the death rate to be in the proportion of about 17 per 1,000 persons living. During the past twenty-six years in Victoria the mortality exceeded 17 per 1,000 seven times, but over the whole period it has averaged below 16 per 1,000. In the last ten years it has never been so high as 16 per 1,000, whilst in six of those years it was below 15 per 1,000, in one of them being even below 14 per 1,000. In 1887 the death rate was 15·70 per 1,000.

The net increase of population in Victoria in 1887, as compared with 1886, was estimated at 33,075, as against 40,953 in New South Wales. The computed total population of Victoria at the close of 1887 was 1,036,119, as compared with 1,003,043 in 1886. The number of males is set down at 550,050, and females at 486,060. On the 31st March, 1888, the estimated population was 1,047,308, showing an increase in the first quarter of the present year of 11,189, 6,946 being males, and 4,243 females.

EDUCATION.—The State educational system of Victoria has been most successful in its operation. The foundation of it is, that secular instruction shall be provided without payment for children whose parents may be willing to accept it, but that, whether accepted or not, satisfactory evidence must be produced that all children are educated up to a given standard. For securing the object sought, it is believed that the system compares favourably with that of any other country in the world. The number of children returned as on the rolls of State schools in 1886, after the system had been in force for thirteen years, was 230,576, and 1,870 schools were open. The parents of children between the ages of six and fifteen are obliged by the "*Education Act*" to cause them to attend school for at least sixty days in each half-year, unless there is some valid reason to prevent them from so doing. The total expenditure on public instruction in 1886-7 was £659,553, of which only £3,549 was paid by parents. Besides the State schools, which are attended by five-sixths of the children under instruction in the colony, there are, according to the latest returns, 691 private schools, attended by 35,811 scholars. Some of these private schools are attached to religious denominations, as many as 175, with 20,854 scholars, being connected with the Roman Catholic Church. Six are called colleges or grammar schools, two of which are connected with the Church of England, two with the Roman Catholic, one with the Presbyterian, and one with the Wesleyan Church. In these, as well as in some of the other private schools, a very high class of education, quite equal to that obtained in the best public schools in England, is given.

The Melbourne University was established under a special Act of the Victorian Legislature, which was

STATISTICS. 113

assented to on the 22nd January, 1853. This Act, as amended by an Act passed in 1881, provides for its endowment by the payment of £9,000 annually out of the general revenue—recently increased by Parliament to £11,000; also, that no religious test shall be required of any one to entitle him to be admitted to the rights and privileges of the institution; also for the election, by the senate, of a council consisting of twenty members, to hold office for five years, of whom not more than three may be members of the teaching staff, and for the election by them, out of their own body, of a chancellor and a vice-chancellor; also for the constitution of a senate, consisting of all male persons who have been admitted to the degree of master or doctor, and for the election by them annually of one of their body as warden, as soon as the superior degrees should amount to not less than one hundred. This number was reached in 1867, and the senate was constituted on the 14th of June of that year. The council are empowered to grant in any faculty, except divinity, any degree, diploma, certificate, or license which can be conferred in any university in the British dominions. Royal letters patent, under the sign-manual of Her Majesty Queen Victoria, were issued on the 14th March, 1859, declaring that all degrees granted, or thereafter to be granted, by the Melbourne University should be recognised as academic distinctions and rewards of merit, and should be entitled to rank, precedence, and consideration in the United Kingdom and in British colonies and possessions throughout the world, just as fully as if they had been granted by any university in the United Kingdom. The foundation stone was laid on the 3rd July, 1854, and the building was opened on the 3rd October of the following year. On the 22nd March,

1880, the University was thrown open to females, and they can now be admitted to all its corporate privileges except as regards the study of medicine. Affiliated to the University is a college in connection with the Church of England, and one in connection with the Presbyterian Church, and a third is in course of being associated with the central seat of learning belonging to the Wesleyan body. The Presbyterian institution is called the Ormond College, after the Hon. Francis Ormond, M.L.C., who has given nearly £25,000 towards its erection and endowment. The University Hall, built at a cost of about £40,000, is called the Wilson Hall, after Sir Samuel Wilson, who contributed the greater portion of the funds for its erection. Since the opening of the University, until 1886, 2,395 students had matriculated, and 1,169 degrees were granted, of which 877 were direct, and 292 *ad eundem.* The students who matriculated in 1886 numbered 154, of whom 18 were females, and the graduates in the same year numbered 124; 249 males and 123 females having passed the matriculation examination.

RAILWAYS.—All the railways in Victoria are the property of the State, whose policy it has been to open up the interior by their means to such an extent that railway communication will keep pace with settlement, be the latter ever so rapid. The consequence is that railways are extending to the most remote parts of the colony. Cheap excursion trains are run weekly, as well as at all holiday seasons, the tickets of the former being available from Friday until Monday, and those of the latter for much longer periods. In June, 1887, 1,880 miles were open for traffic, $236\frac{1}{2}$ miles of which were laid with double lines. The cost of construction, inclusive of rolling-stock, and building a bridge over the Murray to connect with the New

South Wales lines, was over £25,000,000, or an average of about £13,000 per mile. The train mileage during the year was 7,991,378. The total receipts amounted to £1,025,962, and the working expenses to £1,427,116. The net income was equivalent to a return of 4·170 per cent. on the whole capital cost, which shows a substantial surplus, after paying the interest due on the bonds representing the capital expended on the lines. The nominal rate of interest payable on the borrowed capital now averages 4·25 per cent., or £4 5s. per £100. Formerly, the rate was as high as 4¾ per cent., but, owing to the redemption of 6 per cent. debentures and the issue during the years 1883 to 1885 of 4 per cent. debentures in lieu thereof, a reduction of £158,292, upon a total of £482,677, was effected in the annual interest payable.

POST OFFICES.—A very efficient postal system exists in Victoria, and post offices are established throughout the length and breadth of the colony; 1,429 of such institutions now exist, as against 1,007 eight years since. In the same period the letters and newspapers despatched and received in a year increased from 33,000,000 to 55,800,000. The postage on letters to places in any of the Australasian colonies is 2d. per ounce, and on newspapers one halfpenny each. The postage on letters to the United Kingdom is 6d., and on newspapers 1d. Money order offices in Victoria in connection with the post office have been established in 362 places, and the system is being rapidly extended by the opening of fresh offices. Besides the issue and payment of money orders at these places, such orders are issued in favour of Victoria, and Victorian orders are paid, at places in Great Britain and Ireland, and in the various Australasian colonies; also in the United States and Canada; Germany, Belgium, Denmark, and some of the other European countries; Ceylon, India, Straits Settlements, China (including Macao), Japan, the Cape of Good Hope, etc. Postal notes are also issued, for use within the colony, for any amounts not exceeding £1, at charges ranging from ½d. to 3d.

TELEGRAPHS.—Telegraphs in Victoria are Government property, and are worked in connection with the Post Office. Telegraphic communication exists between 420 stations within the colony, and the Victorian lines are connected besides with the lines of New South Wales, and by means of them with Queensland and New Zealand. They are also connected with the lines of South Australia, and by their means with Western Australia, and with the Eastern Archipelago, Asia, Europe and America. They are likewise united with a submarine cable to Tasmania. In 1886 the miles of line along which poles extended numbered 4,094, and the miles of wire 10,111. A considerable extension of the lines, as well as an increase of business, takes place each year. To places within Victoria, telegrams containing not more than six words are sent for 6d., 1d. extra being charged for each additional word. To New South Wales the charge is 1s. for ten words; to South Australia and Tasmania, 2s.; and to Western Australia and Queensland, 3s. To New Zealand ten words are sent for 7s. 6d., each additional word being charged 10d. To England or the continent of Europe, the rate is 10s. 8d. per word; to India it varies from 7s. 11d. to 8s. 4d.; and to the United States, from 12s. 4d. to 13s. 10d. In the case of telegrams to places on the Australian continent, names and addresses are not charged for; to places in Tasmania they are not charged for unless they exceed ten words, but all words above that number are charged for as part of the message. In the

STATISTICS. 117

rase of telegrams to New Zealand, England, the continent of Europe, India, and the United States, the names and addresses of both sender and receiver are charged for as part of the message.

RELIGIOUS STATISTICS.—There being no State religion in Victoria, and no money voted for any religious object, the clergy are supported by the efforts of the denomination to which they are attached. The clergy of the Church of England, with ministers of other bodies, number 1,083, of whom 201 belong to the Church of England, 203 to the Presbyterians, 200 to the Methodists, 129 to the Roman Catholics, 129 to the Salvation Army, 38 to the Bible Christians, 54 to the Independents, 47 to the Baptists, 14 to the Evangelical Lutherans, 5 to the Welsh Calvinists, 21 to the Church of Christ, 2 to the Society of Friends, 3 to the Moravians, 10 to Protestant churches unattached, 1 to the Unitarians, 1 to the Swedenborgians, 16 to the Catholic Apostolic Church, 1 to the Christian Israelites, and 8 to the Jewish Church. The buildings used for public worship throughout Victoria number at present about 4,100, affording accommodation for 552,000 persons.

COST OF LIVING.—The cost of living in Victoria is rather under that in the old country, excepting chiefly the items of house rent, which is high in towns and cities, servants' wages, imported clothing and doctors' fees. In country districts the cost of groceries, tobacco, wines, spirits, &c., is naturally somewhat higher than in Melbourne, and that of agricultural and grazing produce, firewood, &c., somewhat lower than in Melbourne. Prices in Melbourne are quoted as follows:—Bread, per 4lb. loaf, 5d. to 6d.; beef, per lb., 4d. to 10d.; mutton, 1½d. to 5d.; veal, 5d. to 8d.; pork, 6d. to 9d.; lamb, per quarter, 2s. to 3s. 6d.; butter, per lb., 1s. to 2s. 6d.; cheese, 5d. to

1s.; milk, per quart, 5d. to 6d.; flour, £8 to £11 15s. per ton; potatoes, 2s. 6d. to 6s. per cwt.; tea, per lb., 1s. 6d. to 2s. 6d.; coffee, 1s. 3d. to 1s. 6d.; sugar, 2½d. to 3d.; tobacco, 3s. to 6s.; soap, 3d. to 4d.; tallow candles, 4d. to 6d.; sperm candles, 9d. to 1s.; coals, 27s. to 38s. per ton; firewood, 10s. to 14s. 6d.; ale and porter, 8s. to 12s. per dozen; colonial wine, 12s. to 30s. per dozen.

VICTORIA AS A FIELD FOR SETTLEMENT.—There is probably no country in the world that offers such attractions to the working man as Victoria. There, it is not unusual for the agricultural labourer, the artisan and the mechanic to find several masters competing for his services, and outbidding each other in order to obtain them. What is called the eight hours system, founded upon the division of the day into three parts of eight hours each— one to be devoted to labour, one to recreation, and one to rest—has been in existence for the last thirty years, and no employer would venture to ask his men to work a minute longer than the recognised time. Wages are so high and work so constant—the weather being habitually so fine that there is scarcely any broken time—that an industrious man is often able, not only to maintain his family in comfort, but by the exercise of economy to lay by as much as the whole sum of his wages would amount to in England. Free instruction to his children is provided by the State, and, as his boys and girls grow up, plenty of employment offers for them, so that instead of being an expense they soon bring in money.

To women and girls desirous of engaging in domestic service, the colony presents even greater attractions. Wages have been going up steadily for years past, notwithstanding which it is now difficult to get good servants at any wages. Besides the satisfaction of obtaining high remuneration, servants feel that their privileges are greater and the restrictions placed upon them are fewer than in England, whilst, from the value placed upon their services in consequence of the smallness of the supply, they are naturally treated with a kindness and consideration to which many of them had been strangers before coming to Victoria. To professional men, governesses, clerks, shopmen and shopwomen, the certainty of remunerative employment is by no means so absolute as it is to the operative classes, and great caution should be exercised by persons in the old country seeking light employment before deciding to emigrate to Australia. Many succeed beyond their warmest anticipations, whilst others fail utterly. Industry, perseverance, and, it may be added, versatility, will in time conquer many difficulties. The colony presents a large field for male and female instructors, but in this there are many competitors. The failures of society—the dissipated, the drunken, and the idle—had far better not come to the colony. If they do, they will assuredly soon fall into destitution. The field for skilled labour in Victoria has never been better than at present, for during the past year there has been enormous activity in the building trade, largely stimulated by the land "boom," and by a great influx of English money, which is much more profitably invested here than in the Old World. The rights of the working men are carefully watched over by the Council of the Trades Hall, which exerts an important influence in all trade disputes. The education of the working classes in Melbourne has also been liberally provided for by the establishment of a Working Men's College, handsomely endowed by the Hon. Francis Ormond, M.L.C.

www.ingramcontent.com/pod-product-compliance
Lightning Source LLC
Chambersburg PA
CBHW031400160426
43196CB00007B/837